Grieving
the
Death
of a
Father

Grieving

the

Death

of a

Father

HAROLD IVAN SMITH

Broadleaf Books
Minneapolis

Originally published as *On Grieving the Death of a Father* in 1989 by Thomas Nelson, a division of HarperCollins Christian Publishing.

Scripture quotations are from The New King James Version of the Bible, copyright © 1979, 1980, 1982, Thomas Nelson, Inc., Publishers.

The Library of Congress has cataloged the first edition as follows:
LCCN: 94024890
LC Classification: BV4905.2 .S59 1994

Cover design: Lisa Forde
Cover illustration © 2023 Shutterstock; Seamless checkered pattern vector background/1147861472 by Magic Mary

Print ISBN: 979-8-8898-3191-4
eBook ISBN: 979-8-8898-3193-8

This book is dedicated to the memory of my father

ORA PAUL SMITH

BORN September 18, 1911
DIED October 5, 1987

HUSBAND
FATHER
GRANDFATHER
GREAT-GRANDFATHER
FRIEND

"HE PASSED OVER . . .
AND ALL THE TRUMPETS SOUNDED FOR HIM
ON THE OTHER SIDE."
—John Bunyan

CONTENTS

FOREWORD

Harold Ivan Smith

IN THE LAST decade I have often wondered what my dad would think of the world his son lives in. Thirty minutes of national news would leave him shaking his head in dismay. One of his frequent observations was, "Right is right, and wrong is wrong!" But right and *wrong* are fluid words in today's realities.

My mother, on too many occasions, brought me to my senses with this sentence: "Just wait 'til your father gets home." More than once that string of words immediately altered my behavior or attitude. And more than once I pleaded, "Oh, no, don't tell dad," followed with fervent promises.

I have long been intrigued that Father's Day never has had the traction—or commercial impact—of Mother's Day. When I first proposed this book, there was resistance from the marketing folks. Too narrow. Make it about death of *parents,* plural, to increase the market appeal. But a wise editor spoke up: "No! They are different relationships. Grief for a father and for a mother are *not* the same!" Her words carried the day. So, I wrote separate books.

The word *father* covers a variety of relationships: good, bad, absentee, domineering, stern, loving. Rarely have we examined how fathers change or mature or consider that we may have had different fathers at different points in our lives. Mark Twain quipped: "When I was a boy of 14, my father was so ignorant I could hardly stand to have the old man around. But when I got to be 21, I was astonished at how much the old man had learned in seven years." Some grievers have had to balance a before/after around a particular period or event. Some have lamented, "He was never the same after [fill-in-the-blank]." Some have had fathers who were alcoholics or addicts, and that shaped the relationship. Some fathers stopped drinking and were "different"—but that did not always re-balance the scales of memory.

Grief is a particularly demanding terrain for those who were verbally, physically, or sexually abused. Particularly for individuals who grew up in families where "Honor your father and mother" was used as a bludgeon, even long into adulthood.

Some grew up with the influence of television shows like *Father Knows Best*. "Jim Anderson" was always a fatherly fountain of knowledge and wisdom and decency. I don't think he ever lost his temper. And he apparently slept in a white shirt and tie. And then there was Ward Cleaver on *Leave It to Beaver* in contrast to *All in the Family's* grouchy opinionated Archie Bunker. (Plenty laughed, "Yeah, that was my ole man to a tee!") For years Americans followed the single father Ben Cartwright raising three sons on *Bonanza*. Or a single father Lucas McCain who was gentle with his son but lethal with his Winchester rifle on *The Rifleman* or the single dad Jim Newton on the Broken Wheel Ranch on *Fury*. Then *Family Affair* captured the life of uncle-turned-father Bill Davis whose three orphaned nieces and nephews move into his Manhattan townhouse, and, of course, the butler Mr. French was fatherly. Widower Steven Douglas was the wise father raising three boys in *My Three Sons*. And who could forget the wholesome example of widowerer Sheriff Andy Taylor of Mayberry's interaction with Opie?

These television shows not only entertained in prime time but offered images of fathering. Naturally, some of our fathers could not measure up.

In working with families planning funerals and memorial services I have learned to lean in and listen between the lines of their sentences. I listen to what is not said about a father. I have also learned to watch body language of those who are not talking.

In services I have conducted, I have heard some stunning eulogies. I have also heard some diplomatically crafted and rehearsed eulogies, some pointedly brief. I have heard some with some variation of "Well, he did the best he could." Many father's chief role was provider and enforcer rather than nurturer. And the consequences of that role have impacted individuals far beyond childhood. Some children as adults have vowed that they would be better fathers than their fathers had been. Some have been amazed watching their fathers interact with grandchildren and have wondered, "Why he could not have been like that with me?"

Some fathers minimized words in interactions with children: "My house/my rules" or "As long as you live under my roof . . ." And many children heard the default response: "Because I said so, that's why!" Or "If I have to get up and come in there . . ." Too many have memories of slammed doors and abruptly ended conversations and eerie silences.

Many lived under an inhibiting double whammy: "Honor your father" from the famous Ten Commandments tag teamed with the admonition "Speak no ill of the dead."

Some grievers have compounded their grief by keeping "the grand jury" in session. Some sons and daughters can always get a fresh indictment against their fathers for real or imagined behaviors.

Some grievers have spent years, decades, trying to win a father's approval. Some have lived in the shadow of the favored son or daughter. No few have married prematurely to get away from a father.

Some have suffered under rigid Christian fundamentalist fathers who were quick—too quick—to demonstrate the "biblical" mandate, or *their* interpretation of "Spare the rod and spoil the child" (Proverbs 13:24).

Grief can be fueled by the "father I *never had*, the father I *once had*, the father I *should have had* . . ."

Some grievers have "lost" fathers to dementia or Alzheimer's long before biological death.

Some grievers have grieved more for stepfathers or grandfathers or uncles who became positive father figures. Some individuals have been blessed with a father-in-law as surrogate father. Some have grieved more for a father-in-law than for a father but feel a sting of guilt for that reality.

Some have had the ragged experience of a father who "went off the deep end" whether in criminal acts, addiction, or political or religious fanaticism. Or the father who was "never home" or was a workaholic who missed ball games, dance recitals, and plays.

Some, as adults, have had to limit time around fathers or have learned to dodge the "landmines" in conversation, whether religious or political. No few have snapped, "Dad!" or abruptly announced, "Gotta go. . ." despite a "but you just got here."

Some grieving for a father have been ambushed by a PMD, or *postmortem discovery*: other children they knew nothing about or never suspected, jail sentences, previous unacknowledged marriages, affairs. Settling an estate—or journeying through probate—can lead to discovering the money "is not there" or another sibling "got more" or "took" more.

Some grief for fathers has been complicated by second or third marriages or a girlfriend's presence; some have resented a new wife or girlfriend who "poisoned" their relationship or limited time with a father. Some have seen a father go through a metamorphis in a new relationship.

In conducting some funerals, I have to be a diplomat shuffling between children from a first marriage and children from the second marriage (or no marriage). Or negotiating the structure of a service and who would sit where or ride in which car. In one case, separate visitations were necessary because the man's children would not be in the "same room"—even in a funeral home. And I have heard the angry stories of those "left out" of obituaries—published or in the service itself.

Indeed, some have questioned having a funeral. Some have expressed it bluntly: "Just get him in the ground!" Or there have been tense conversations or arguments about "how much to spend on dad?" And I have had services in which a son or daughter "did not show." (One said that 10:00 a.m. was "just too early.") And I spent time in the lobby trying to talk an only son into staying for his father's funeral. (He left midway through the service.)

The distinguished thanatologist Colin Murray Parkes offered sage insight that should be carved in granite: "Anything that continually allows the person to avoid or suppress . . . pain can be expected to prolong the course of mourning" (p. 173; 1972, *Bereavement studies of grief in adult life*. NY: International Universities Press).

Some grievers respond, "Oh, my father died a long time ago" or "he died when I was a child." But there is no statute of limitations on grief.

On occasion after individuals have told me their father was "an s.o.b.," I have responded: "Well, at least, he did one thing right." "And what is *that*!?" some have snapped. "Ah, he brought you into the world. And the world would be a very different place without you."

Some complain, "I can't seem to get over the grief." My stock answer is, "Have you gotten *into* the grief?" Make no mistake: there are opportunities to do "lite" grief. Thorough grief for a father is an investment in yourself.

INTRODUCTION

I HAVE LONG been impressed with the ability of death to make shambles of all our carefully ordered priorities. A single phone call—whether local or long distance—suddenly takes from us one whom we have known, loved, hated, touched, fed, hurt, surprised, photographed, cleaned up after, and bought presents for. In an instant we're taken from the present tense and some glimmer of hope for the future back to the past tense. Period.

We grieve in a society that goes to elaborate technological means to joust with the old adversary death. A society that has no more chance of really defeating death today than our ancestors did a generation, a century, or a millenia ago.

Today's society responds to death with tasteful sympathy cards, sprays of glads and carnations, casseroles or other food for the bereaved, or all too brief moments in a funeral parlor or church. There. Miss Manners would approve. We have responded to death in a respectable manner.

Death is even cut and dried in personnel manuals and policies at work. They spell out the rules: we can have one day off for this death and three days off for that death. "Let's see. Your father died? So sorry. When can you be back to work?"

No wonder we have such a struggle learning the lesson that death would teach us. No wonder we have such a lack of insight into the comfort God would give us. There's too much in our way.

Somehow this book has come to you—perhaps as a gift, or after someone has scribbled the title on a piece of paper and said, "Read this!" or after finding it while browsing through the grief section in the library. Yet you probably wouldn't be interested in reading this book if you hadn't had a father who had existed and in a specific moment of passion or pleasure or delicate communion shared the tiniest hint of life with your birth mother. Nine months before you ever breathed, you had a father.

And now your father has died. . . .

Make no mistake about it—the death of a father causes a very significant wound! Some of us tend the wound; some of us ignore it. But, surprisingly, the wound is not that our father died and by his death our world is forever altered or changed. No, the wound is that the world around us acknowledged the death for one brief moment and then skipped merrily on its way. The death of our father! An event of such consequence to us! And yet soon, too soon, even those near and dear to us forgot. They stopped saying, "Sorry to hear about your dad," or "How's your mom adjusting?" or especially, "How's it going with you?" The wound of apathy, of indifference—that's the truly significant wound.

Now, at the same time we struggle with the wound, we also face a new dilemma. Thomas Moore acknowledged the dilemma in *Soul Mates*: "Death doesn't erase a relationship; it simply places it in a different context." Yes, but what context? That's the dilemma we face now. What is the father-child relationship now?

Perhaps you, like me, learned the nuances of the commandment "Honor your father and mother. . ." early in life. But what "honor" meant when our fathers were alive is quite different from what it means now.

Now we have new ways to honor our father and his memory. For example, we can:

- keep his picture within sight
- visit his grave
- remember his birth date or death date
- give a church a charitable gift in his memory
- treasure the gifts he gave us or the objects he left us

- share some of his personal items with our children or other close family members
- tell stories about his life and retell the stories he told
- drop a line to his old friends, coworkers, or alumni paper
- assemble a scrapbook of pictures and activities he found meaningful
- remember his personal laugh, his sigh, his smell, his mannerisms, his strength, his very being, him.

Remembrances of a father after these moments catch the griever by surprise. Recently I noticed my father's watch in a dark corner of my safety deposit box. Its presence there exemplified the great value I had assigned it. As I turned the watch in my hand, I remembered my father's commitment to being on time . . . always . . . if not early.

Remembrances help heal. As a storyteller, I lead a group called People with Grief. Grieving people attend the group sessions to tell stories about those they have lost and to listen to similar stories of fellow grievers. Everyone takes a place in a circle of chairs. Everyone talks. Everyone listens. Stories. Memories. Glimpses. Jarred into consciousness by another's words. Punctuated with tears, silences, laughter, or other emotions from the rich palate of the soul.

In *On Grieving the Death of a Father*, I have woven into one resource book glimpses from my personal recollections of my father's life, plus recollections of others who have experienced the death of a father.

Make no mistake—your father's death affects you regardless of the status of your relationship with him at the time of his death. In ways apparent and not so apparent, his death shapes you. While reading this book there may be times when you need to put it down and simply listen to your own heart, to turn off the television and recognize your personal memories, to take off your headphones and rehearse your own stories, to close your eyes and say a prayer. Look through your life for the telltale lifeprints of the one you call father. Thank God for them. Thank God for him.

Finally, never be ashamed of your grief. The preacher of Ecclesiastes tells us that there is a time to mourn, a time to grieve. Our Lord wept in grief. Grief is natural after a loss. Embrace your grief. Work through it. By doing so you honor your father.

Harold Ivan Smith

FIRST THOUGHTS

When you lose your father, you lose your best friend.

George Bush

The Phone Call

ONE EARLY MORNING phone call left me without a dad. *Without.* That word ricocheted through my heart.

6:45 A.M. I had gotten up early to get a jump on the paperwork and bills and telephone calls and correspondence. Two weeks on the road had made shambles of my desktop.

The phone rang. A collect call from my niece. No "How are you?" No "Sorry to be calling so early."

"We've lost Pap-Paw," she said.

I was annoyed. "How could you lose Pap-Paw? He's in room 302 at Methodist Hospital," I snapped.

"No," she said. "We *lost* him."

It hit me.

"Is your dad there?" I asked, as if my brother would disclaim what she had just said to me. I had never heard tears in my brother's voice until that moment. "He's gone, Harold."

And, as men do, we talked details. When? What happened? He answered my questions before I could phrase them as I stared through the blinds at my backyard where squirrels and rabbits were making their last walk of the night or first walk of the morning. Suddenly, I was commending myself that I had not first reached for my jogging shoes, that I had decided to move a little paperwork before my morning run. I think it was easier on my family to be able to tell me immediately.

Finally, I had to ask for one more voice to tell me, the voice that would make it "official," but a voice I didn't want to hear, because if Mother said it, the words could not be taken back. I had to hear it from three generations that morning.

"Where's Mother?"

"She's right here."

And suddenly she was right there. Simultaneously in the hospital and in my study.

"He's gone." Although I had heard her cry before, never had I heard her voice sound like this.

And now I felt that the writer son was supposed to say something everyone would remember. But after a few minutes of silence, I gave up and said, fighting back the tears, "He'll never suffer anymore."

"He's in a better world," Mother added in a tone that implied she wished in that moment she could join him.

We talked details. How soon could I get there? "By afternoon," I promised. I would have to call my travel agent, and I knew I would have to wait until the bank opened. Suddenly, all those details that are always at the front of your brain when you don't need them wouldn't cooperate. I couldn't remember when the bank or the travel agency opened.

Somehow, although I knew it would happen, had to happen—how much more could he stand?—I had not suspected that it would feel like this, an ache I could not describe that crisp October morning of 1987.

There would be no replacement. Dad was a one-of-a-kind father. A one-of-a-kind good man, the kind the world could not replace.

He and I were as different as night and day. We had never voted the same way. Even if we chose the same party, we chose different wings of that party.

Yet we were also alike. We were both strongly committed to our faith, which was a vital part of our lives. I was my father's son, for sure.

Although it was before dawn, I called friends and cried out my anguish.

Fortunately, not one of them said, "Do you know what time it is?" Instead they listened. And they cried with me. Grown men. Someday—sooner than any of us maybe knew—the roles would be reversed. They would dial my number. And I would listen to their anguish.

Later that morning, on the plane to Louisville, I had a crazy feeling that this was all a dream. I realized that I would not believe that Daddy was dead until I got there, until I saw him. It would prove to be easier for most of my family since they had gotten to see him "dead" immediately. That would be the way they would remember him.

I did not know and fortunately would not know until I got off the plane later that afternoon that I would not be able to see Dad that day. The funeral home that Daddy and I had discussed was full. They could not accommodate us until the next evening at 4 P.M.

That only made it tougher on me. He was dead but not dead until I saw him dead.

I kept busy.

But the calls—business calls that *had* to be made because I had been on the road for two weeks—seemed out of sync. "How are you?"

"Not very well."

"Oh?"

"My dad *just* died."

And they all said, "I'm sorry." Some because that was what they were supposed to say.

I found myself—a grown man—wanting to be comforted. I had told the bank teller, the dizzy blonde at the cleaners.

I found myself wishing that I had said, "Daddy, I love you," on that last phone call yesterday. Instead, Dad and I had spent what would be our last conversation talking about the weather, my travel plans, and who had visited him that day. But then I didn't know it was the last time I would talk to him. In fact, it really wasn't much of a call from my point of view. I ended up saying, "Daddy, I wish I knew what to say to make it better."

That was dumb. I make my living with words, speaking and writing. Thousands of people read and listen to me each year. Why didn't I have some words for my dad in that moment?

But maybe it was enough for him that his youngest son had called.

I found myself asking why, after that call, when I had sensed the seriousness of his medical status, I hadn't said to the airline ticket agent, "Forget that schedule. Book me to Louisville." If I had been there—staying at my parents' house—I could have gotten my mother to the hospital a few moments earlier, and she might have seen Dad before he died. But she had to wait for my brother to come and get her.

Why did I say to myself in that split second of quandary, I can always go to Louisville later in the week if his condition gets worse? Why did that sound so rational to me at that moment?

I wouldn't have seen him alive anyway. I would have arrived too late to go to the hospital. Now I can understand my logic, but in those first moments after *the call*—and that's the way I will always remember it—I kept wondering, why did I put schedule ahead of my father?

Why is it that at such moments words like *should, ought, shouldn't, maybe, perhaps* keep bouncing around inside our hearts?

It would only be later—one of those nights as my mother and I sat talking—that she said she had known he was already "gone" when the hospital called and said, "You'd better come."

And although I had thought about how I would feel when Daddy died, reality seemed far more crude and rude that October morning. In moments, my priorities lay in shambles. With one phone call.

My father had *died.* That was the word I insisted on using. That word had to be used.

Daddy was not "lost."

Daddy had not "passed away."

Daddy had not "expired."

Daddy had died.

Avi Met

In Hebrew it means: My father died. Three of the most painful words in the vocabulary of humankind. No explanations, no theory, no formulas can lessen the pain we experience. We have lost our father, and that is one of life's profoundest losses. For some of us, the death of a father is life's deepest insult. It reminds us of our own vulnerability. Only those who die before their father escape these feelings and saying these words.

Perhaps your experience with your father's death has been something like mine. That's what this book is all about. It's one son sharing his road map with other pilgrims who have lost their fathers and are desperately trying to make sense of the experience.

Grief is not a linear path, a straight line from point A to point B. Hardly.

It's a journey with many right turns, left turns, U-turns, and detours. But never forget it is the journey we all make. I grew up in Kentucky and remember the old folk song, "You gotta walk that lonesome valley; You gotta walk it by yourself."

No, you don't.

The theme running through this book is, *You are not alone.* That is stated first through passages written by noted personalities. You will meet Dwight David Eisenhower, who, thousands of miles from home, in a tent in North Africa, grieved for his father. And Lech Walesa, whose dad died from the ravages of years in a forced labor camp. And Roger Wilkins, who buried his father in a "blacks only" cemetery. I chose these individuals to show the wide range of experiences and emotions and behaviors after a father's death. As you read their stories, you will realize: *I am not alone. Others have walked this path before me, and their experiences will help me to understand mine.*

Second, the theme "You are not alone" is stated in passages of Scripture that say, "God understands your grief."

On Grieving the Death of a Father is divided into four major sections, one for each passage in the natural course of grief: the passing, the burying, the mourning, and the remembering. Each of the sections has these components: my own reflections, passages by noted personalities, quotations worth remembering, Scriptures, a hymn, and formal and informal prayers that comfort.

This book is not designed to be read in one sitting, although you can do so if you wish. Rather, the grieving reader is like a traveler on a long, cross-country drive, who reaches into the glove compartment and pulls out his or her trusted road map to find another resting point on the journey.

I suggest that you place this book by your bedside. On your desk. In your briefcase. Keep it handy for the moments when those *avi met* feelings return. And feel free to read this book in any order you choose. You may even find the need to reread sections.

Simply, "You gotta walk this lonesome valley. . . ." But you don't have to walk it alone. Let's make the journey together. . . .

1

THE PASSING

When he left us, it was as if a green tree had fallen in the forest, and left a lonesome place against the sky.

Anonymous

I Wonder If He Knew

I'VE WONDERED IF my father knew, in that split second of final pain, that this would be the last pain he would ever experience.

I've wondered if he knew that my mother would get to the hospital too late and would feel bad about it, not just for a few hours but for the rest of her life.

I've wondered if he knew that there would be no more "I thought I was a goner for sure's." So many nights when it looked bleak, he had pulled through to eat breakfast at dawn. How many times had we made those calls saying, "He pulled through; it was an answer to prayer."

I've wondered about the many "close calls": perhaps his mansion on the other side wasn't ready. So he had to wait in a lobby called pain. Or maybe he had a klutz for a death angel.

I've wondered if he was at all surprised when, in that split second of final pain, the tardy white-winged one said, "Smitty, this one ain't a dress rehearsal. It's a go."

I've wondered if in that split second of final pain, the vibrant yell of a boy released from school for summer recess erupted from deep within his spirit.

I've wondered what he felt—in that split second of final pain—when he felt the first breath of peace and knew that it would last forever.

Curiosity

You can count on it. Some folks will want to know more than the obituary reported. That is, about the very end. They really want to ask, "How did he face death?" For some it is understandable. They have seen people who were in obscene pain, wracked with torment; others who died in their sleep, peacefully; and a few who "never knew what hit them." In such conversations, some people will even tell you how they want to die: "When my time comes, I wanna go. . . ."

In my dad's case, the official report said, "Heart attack." Simply, he got up on Monday morning, as he had every Monday morning for three years, to get ready to go to kidney dialysis. That medical process had kept him alive.

My dad was a man of habit. He always got up early. Even on vacation. Even on Sundays. Even on holidays. Even in retirement. Oh, once in a while, he might sleep until 6 A.M. My earliest recollections of Dad are of hearing him stir before dawn, making a pot of coffee, listening to WHAS radio.

Part of his morning ritual was reading Scripture. He always read through the Bible every year. You could leaf through his Bible and tell where he had read: he left markings beside certain passages. And his Bible had that worn look.

That particular October morning, he read. And he prayed. Now for my father, prayer was not some formalistic exercise in Elizabethan English with all the *th* endings. Hardly. My dad talked to the Lord just as he talked to everyone, in a conversational tone. And he simply expressed the concerns of his heart. I am certain that most of those days he mentioned me to the Lord, because he had a healthy skepticism about airline safety that I often dismissed with an "Oh, Dad!"

While I can't prove anything, this is what I think happened. That morning as he waited, he and the Lord were having the best conversation and just walking as they talked. Finally, the Lord said, "Paul, it's closer to my house than it is to yours. Why don't you just come on home with me?"

And in a split second, I think my father said yes and stepped into eternity.

Some would say he "passed away." Or he "expired." I think he *stepped* into eternity. And I doubt if he looked back.

As I faced the funeral and those first days after his death, I began to look for consolation from the experience of others who can say *avi met*. I especially appreciated the stories people told me about my father. Some filled in gaps in my knowledge of my dad. Others made me appreciate his uniqueness. And a few only stimulated my grief and sense of loss.

Perhaps because I am a writer, I turned to books, particularly biographies. I wanted more than pious phrases and promises. I wanted accounts of how others had made the journey. I was not disappointed. For I found words and phrases and stories that met particular needs.

Recollections of Fathers' Deaths

Many adult sons and daughters will make that long trip home that I made after my dad died. Jimmy Roosevelt, son of former president Franklin Delano Roosevelt, made such a trip. In this account he describes his own journey and the particular pain that accompanied it. His father died on April 12, 1945, at age sixty-three.

Jimmy Roosevelt was thirty-eight at the time. . . .

Two hours and ten minutes after he was stricken, father expired. Mother and Anna [his sister] were notified. The news was flashed around the world. Halfway across the world, I got the word. In a short while, a personal message reached me through official communications. Mother sent each of her sons the same message:

DARLINGS: FATHER SLEPT AWAY THIS AFTERNOON. HE DID HIS JOB TO THE END AS HE WOULD WANT YOU TO DO. BLESS YOU. ALL OUR LOVE, MOTHER.

I thought then, as I sat alone awhile in my room, that father was as much a victim of the war as any soldier who had been killed in battle. I think now how the Civil War aged Abraham Lincoln, how World War I wasted Woodrow Wilson, how World War II exhausted my father. . . . If they outlasted the wars, as my father did not, how little was left of them, and how little time left for them. The presidency makes brutal demands on men in the best of times.

The presidency also makes brutal demands on the sons. Roosevelt naturally wanted to be with his family in New York. But other sailors had lost their fathers and had stayed in battle. Could he be an exception? And if he did fly home, wouldn't it be seen as just another example of favoritism for the Roosevelt boys?

Admiral Davis came in to see me to ask if there was anything he could do for me. We got word that the official ceremonies were to be held in Washington and the burial at Hyde Park. I told the admiral I would like to get back for the funeral if possible. He said he would do everything he could. Within four hours I was on a plane. But I was nine thousand miles away, and the complicated travel plan called for me to make one stop en route to Guam, change planes, stop at Wake en route to Honolulu, on to San Francisco, then cross-country to New York, and upstate to Hyde Park. I knew I could not make the ceremonies, but I hoped to make the burial—until head winds slowed my schedule.

I wanted to be with him one last time. I had known all along how much I admired him. But I did not realize until then how much I loved him. I was sorry I had never said it in so many words, though I think he knew. As father and son we'd not had the opportunity to be close most of my life, but working with him and for him the last few

years before the war, we had come close to one another. I was grateful
for that at least.

What did the grieving son think about as he flew home to New York?

I would like to be able to say that I thought about what father's
death would mean to the world, but I thought only of what it would
mean to mother, to me, to my brothers and my sister. Our lives had
gone down one road for so long that we knew no other way. Now our
lives would be altered, to follow another course.

*Unfortunately, nature did not cooperate. At one point he had word
sent to his mother that he would not make the burial. Mrs. Roosevelt sug-
gested that he meet her in New York City and he could ride back on the
train to Washington, D.C. Because of his fatigue, he checked his bags at
Grand Central Station and decided to walk along Park Avenue.*

It was late afternoon on a sunny April day. I was in uniform and
no one noticed me or recognized me as I strolled distractedly along the
avenue until I got to Eightieth Street. . . .
Suddenly, a cab pulled to the curb alongside me, the driver got
out, rushed over to me and asked if I was who he thought I was. I said
that I was Jimmy Roosevelt if that was who he meant. He said it was,
and he started to tell me how much he had admired my father. His
passenger leaned out and said he'd hired the driver to take him home,
not to talk to some [expletive] about that [expletive] Roosevelt, who
would have been better off dead long ago.

*How did the grieving son deal with such an insult on the day of his
father's funeral?*

I had long since hardened myself to endure the most unfeeling
of insults, but at this time it was too tough to take. I excused myself

to the cabbie, shook his hand and thanked him. He had started to cry. As I walked away, I turned back in time to see him haul his passenger, a well-dressed Wall Street type, out of the cab and deposit him on the curb. Then he drove away.

My Parents: A Differing View, 285–287.

After my dad died, I struggled with guilt about not being at my father's deathbed. In the next months, I saw that other sons and daughters had felt the same way—like former president of the United States Dwight David Eisenhower; *Metropolitan Opera soprano and later general manager of the New York Opera* Beverly Sills; *Pope John XXIII; and female vocalist* Norma Zimmer.

Dwight Eisenhower *was in Africa as deputy to the General Marshall for Operations of the US Army on March 9, 1942, when he learned that his father had died at seventy-nine years of age.*

Dwight Eisenhower was fifty-one years old at the time. . . .

When the word came that he was gone . . . it was not possible for me to leave. But it was not possible for me to go ahead with business-as-usual. I closed the door to my office and sat thinking about the life we had all had together. . . .

March 11, 1942. My father was buried today. I've shut off all business and visitors for thirty minutes—to have that much time, by myself, to think of him. He had a hill life. He left six boys . . . and fortunately . . . Mother survives. . . . He was a just man, well liked, a thinker. He was undemonstrative, quiet, modest, and of exemplary habits—he never used alcohol or tobacco.

His finest monument is his reputation in Abilene and Dickinson Co. . . . His word has been his bond and accepted as such. Because of it, all central Kansas helped me secure an appointment to West Point in 1911, and thirty years later, it did the same for my son John. I'm proud he was my father. My only regret is that it was always so difficult to let him know the depth of my affection for him.

Later that evening Eisenhower added to his journal,

I have felt terribly. I should like so much to be with my mother these few days. But we're at war. And war is not soft—it has no time to indulge even the deepest and most sacred emotions. I loved my Dad. . . .

Quitting work now—7:30 P.M. I haven't the heart to go on tonight.

At Ease: Stories I Tell My Friends, 304–305.

Beverly Sills's parents decided not to tell her that her father, Morris Silverman, had cancer. In the months after his death, Beverly wondered about this decision and finally resolved the question in her own mind. Her father died in 1948 at fifty-three years of age.

Beverly was nineteen years old at the time. . . .

My parents never told me about Papa's lung cancer or the desperate nature of the operations he was about to undergo, which were a last-ditch effort to contain the spread of his cancer.

Just before the operations were to take place, I was offered $300 plus my passage to sing four concerts on a thirty-eight day Moore-McCormach Line cruise to Buenos Aires, Argentina. My mother and father both told me to take the job. Papa was still going to be in pain when I got back, they told me, but eventually he'd recover. They said the doctors were fairly convinced he had tuberculosis, but that still wasn't a certainty. So off I went to Buenos Aires, and I had a wonderful time.

My father died five days before I returned to New York. He was only fifty-three years old. My parents and my father's doctor had all decided it was wiser for me to go to South America than to stay home and see Papa waste away. For a long time, I felt an enormous sense of guilt about having left my father's side when he was so sick.

I frequently tell myself that I'm very much like my father, and that if I were gravely ill, I'd also send away a child of mine.

Beverly: An Autobiography, 44–45.

Angelo Roncalli, *who became* Pope John XXIII, *was serving in Istanbul in the summer of 1935 when his father, Giovanni Roncalli, died. His father was eighty-one years old.*

Roncalli was fifty-four years old at the time. . . .

. . . a cable arrived telling Roncalli of the death of his father. The deep love he felt for the simple, good man who had been so naively proud of his son's position made a torment of Roncalli's grief. Although Giovanni Roncalli was eighty-one years old and had lived a full and happy life, his son was heartbroken not to have been able to be with him—to hold his hand once more and to give him the consolation of the sacraments. As soon as possible, Roncalli returned to Sotto il Monte to comfort his mother, and found the sweet, sad consolation of praying at his father's grave.

What more could he do?

Hatch, *A Man Named John—The Life of Pope John XXIII*, 96.

Norma Zimmer *was a popular female vocalist on Lawrence Welk's television show. Her relationship with her father, who was divorced from her mother, had been strained, yet there seemed to be signs of healing between father and daughter. Her father, Peter (Huseby) Larsen, died alone in July of 1966.*

When Norma's father did not show up for work, her husband, Randy, went to look for him. . . .

"Did you find him?"

Sadly Randy replied, "Yes, honey, I found him."

"Where is he?" I asked.

"I found him slumped over the steering wheel in his car. He was parked in the lot at Ralph's [a supermarket], a bag of groceries next to him."

"Is he—?"

"He's dead."

I was devastated. What a terrible way to die—alone, perhaps in pain. I went to my room and threw myself on the bed, sobbing. If only I could have been with him.

I learned that dad had probably been there a day and a half. He had been dead more than twenty-four hours. How he could have been there that long without being noticed remains a mystery. He had had a heart attack.

Mother accepted the news without a trace of emotion. No tears, no trembling of the jaw. She did say, "What a shame he had to die like that." I felt she was glad he was out of her life.

Mother didn't want to go to the funeral. She finally went to please me. I tried to hold back the tears because I knew if I started to sob I wouldn't be able to stop. When a few tears squeezed past my swollen lids and trickled down my cheeks, mother leaned over and whispered to me, "I should have brought a towel," referring to the many times she had gone into her bathroom to get me a towel when she knew I was going to cry. Then she would toss it in my lap and say, "Now cry."

My mother shed no tears of her own for dad. She sat dry-eyed and hard-lipped through the service.

We buried him at Memory Gardens in La Habra. As I stood looking at the grave, I hoped dad was in heaven. Since coming to California, he had become a student of the Bible. He had never told me he knew the Lord, but I believed he did.

Mother made me promise her that when she died we wouldn't bury her in the same cemetery with dad.

Norma, 266–269.

Some daughters and sons do not know that their father has died until weeks or months after the fact

Natan Sharansky *(an internationally recognized spokesman for the dissident Moscow Jews who wanted to emigrate to Israel in the mid-seventies) was confined as a political prisoner in a Soviet gulag when his father, Boris, died on January 20, 1980, Natan's birthday.*

Natan was thirty-two years old at the time. He knew something significant had happened when Captain Mavrin, head of the political section of the prison, came to his cell...

He said, "Sharansky, I have a very unpleasant telegram for you."

I immediately understood everything, although I didn't want to believe it. No, I told myself, Mavrin didn't say anything, it only seemed that he did. I took the telegram with trembling hands.

My dearest son! Yesterday, on January 20, Papa passed away. Please bear this sorrow as bravely as I did. Natasha and I are well, and are with you all the time. I kiss you affectionately. Mama.

It can't be true—it's a KGB provocation! But no matter what I told myself, I knew I no longer had a father. By some miracle I managed to control myself, and in a strange, hoarse, and dead voice, I asked, "May I send a telegram to my mother?"

I heard the standard reply: "Write a request to the head of the prison and we'll see."

I went to my bed, turned toward the wall, and cried silently—for the second and last time since my arrest. The first time was after the trial, but those were tears of relief, while these were the tears of a helpless child. I suddenly felt alone, that nobody and nothing was protecting me. The days that followed were perhaps the most difficult of all my years in the Gulag.

By this time Yosef had been moved to a cell across from mine and we devised yet another means of communication: while pretending to sing Hebrew prayers, we were able to send brief messages to each other. The day after I received Mama's telegram, Yosef sang me belated birthday greetings. But instead of singing back, I simply said *Avi met* (My father died).

Fear No Evil, 270.

Many sons and daughters are able to be with their parents when they die. This can be either a blessing, as it was to Roberta Donovan *(a Western freelance writer and former newspaper editor), or a period of torture, as it was to novelist* Harry Petrakis, *who watched his father suffer a slow, painful death.*

Roberta Donovan's *father, Ike Messier, died on September 7, 1971, at the age of seventy-nine*

Roberta had celebrated her fiftieth birthday with her father in the hospital three days before his death. Roberta recalls the special gift her father gave her at that time:

We both knew, my dad and I, that he was slipping from this mortal life. We didn't speak of it; we didn't need to put it into words. Instead, we grinned at each other, as we had always done, and I said, "Sing me a French song, Dad."

And lying there in the hospital's cardiac unit, with his heart monitor beating time, Dad sang me one last song. The singing wasn't the important thing. What mattered was the love we shared, the unspoken communication of our spirits. Our mutual pride in his French-Canadian heritage was a part of that; hence the song.

By singing to me, Dad made of even this most somber occasion a joyful memory. It was his way. His almost eighty years were spent in thoughtfully lifting the load of others.

I can still remember as a little girl, having Dad swing me onto his broad shoulders and carry me down the street because the snow was too deep for my chubby little legs. It was typical of how he always smoothed life's path for me.

But of all my memories of my father, I cherish most the way he always understood me. He seemed to sense how I felt, my disappointments and my dreams. When I was in high school, he somehow managed to scrape up the money to buy me a portable typewriter, because he knew how much it meant to me to have one.

I sensed once more that loving understanding as I stood by Dad's bed, holding his hand as he bid me farewell with that silly little

French song. It was one more unspoken message, telling me that he loved me.

I don't know the words to the song, or even its title, but I know what it was saying. In Dad's gentle way, he was telling me, "Don't weep, honey, for this, too, is a part of life and I'll be waiting for you over there."

Letter to author.

Harry Petrakis *watched his father, Mark E. Petrakis (former rector of St. Constantine Hellenic Orthodox Church in Chicago), suffer, as I watched mine.*

Mark Petrakis died on Memorial Day 1951.

Harry was twenty-seven at the time. . . .

There were many times, especially as the weeks went on, when drugs and pain rendered him inert and silent, I'd sit beside his bed, trying to find something to say to reassure him and myself, yearning to leave so I would not have to see his veins, swollen and purple along his wrists, the pulse that wiggled like a small dark worm in his forehead. Worst of all was the smell of decay like a rank mist from his body. I couldn't understand how my mother endured the endless hours she spent with him. After sitting with him for a while, I'd lie to him about an appointment or an errand that prevented my staying longer. He never complained about my departures, never tried to detain me, but urged me to go and meet my obligations.

Sometimes I grew angry at the measure of his suffering, resenting his acceptance of the cathartic qualities of pain. When I lamented what he was being forced to endure, he reproached me softly.

"I have done things, harbored thoughts, spoken words for which I am ashamed," he told me. "Now God gives me a chance to clean myself of these poisons."

In accordance with that conviction he sent for men from the parish, men he had denounced as his enemies. He forgave them and asked each of them to forgive him.

Still incredibly, he clung to life.

On those days he felt a little stronger, he enjoyed sitting by the window in his room, looking across the roofs of the buildings toward the faintly visible spire and belltower of the old church that had been sold. Since he no longer had the strength to walk, on these occasions I lifted him from the bed and carried him to the armchair by the window. His wasted body seemed to float in my arms.

On such a day, alone with him in the room, as I carried him the few feet from his bed to the armchair, he rested his cheek against my cheek. "As I once carried you in my arms," he said softly, "now you carry me."

He died a few days later, quietly in his sleep, a short while after my mother had left the hospital to come home.

Reflections: A Writer's Life, A Writer's Work, 92–94.

I was an adult when my father died. Some people suffer from the death of a father they can scarcely remember. One such person is Lech Walesa, *Polish Solidarity leader, whose father, Boleslaw, died in 1945 at the age of thirty-seven.*

Boleslaw's premature death occurred after two years of forced labor in a German camp near Lipno. The prisoners there suffered from bitter cold. When they fell asleep with their heads against the wall, their hair froze and stuck to the wood. Boleslaw's medical condition deteriorated from these poor conditions. He came home to die before his son was old enough to know him:

When he at last came home for good, he was utterly exhausted, suffered frequent hemorrhages, and was already full of regrets for a life he felt was drawing to a close. He was to remain with us barely two months.

In May, 1945, Uncle Stanislaw also returned from the camp. He began working again straightway, living at Uncle Izydor's house and eating at ours. Father's condition was so serious that the priest was called to administer the last rites. On the very brink of death, he had waited for Uncle Stanislaw's return so that he could die in peace, repeating that he couldn't give up his soul before entrusting us [the family] into his safekeeping. He made Stanislaw swear solemnly that he would take care of us, and he entreated my mother to look after Edward and me, stressing that one day she would be proud of me. He was lucid right up until the end. About four in the morning, while we children were asleep, with Grandmother Kaminska watching over us, he calmly asked my mother to wake us and send us out. And so he died. He was buried at Sobowo. I couldn't go to the funeral, which was attended by the rest of the family along with numerous people from the neighborhood: I was eighteen months old at the time.

A year later Mother decided to marry Stanislaw.

A Way of Hope, 26–27.

The death of a natural father is traumatic. But thousands of sons and daughters, like comedian Art Linkletter, do not even know the identity of their biological fathers. They have been raised by adopted fathers. The loss is just as great.

Art Linkletter was adopted by the Reverend John Fulton, who died in 1944 at the age of eighty-three.

Art was thirty-two years old at the time. . . .

In 1944, when Father was eighty-three years old, he suffered the first serious illness of his life. He was stricken with pneumonia, and he fussed and fretted because he had to stay in bed. He always had remarkable physical strength, and I could almost see him shaking his fist at the four walls that held him and angrily telling the doctor that no puny virus could lick him. But now the old vigor was gone, and the fight was lost. He died quietly in his sleep, an isolated man who had never quite caught up with the times.

Art Linkletter had offered to buy his parents a house in Pomona or Los Angeles, but they chose to live in a small two-bedroom, upstairs apartment in Pasadena. They rarely read the newspapers and "almost never went beyond the periphery of their insular little world." They had no idea of their son's fame.

I never doubted that he loved me, in his own unfathomable way. But I think I was little more than an image he had built into his mind. . . .

Often at the death of a loved one, we sorrow at the blows life has dealt him, at his frustrated dreams, his unreached goals, and we wish he might have had a second chance. But I could feel none of these regrets for Father Linkletter. He had been a preacher and a humble cobbler whose happiness in life was doing his work well. He never found reason to stop loving his fellow man, or to stop helping him. He had so often shown us the power of simple goodness, and at all times he had been sustained by complete confidence in the justness of his God. He would not have altered the course of his life in the slightest degree.

And so I could not grieve for him.

I could only know that I was a better man for what he gave, and that I would be less with him gone.

Confessions of a Happy Man, 179.

As I read through passages written by sons and daughters, I found different responses to their father's death—from syndicated humor columnist Lewis Grizzard's *submerged grief to author* Frederick Buechner's *amazement at his father's suicide to author* Tim Hansel's *feelings of love and peace*

Lewis Grizzard, Jr., *is a professional humorist who makes people laugh. Yet there is a tender side that few people see. That side became evident after the death of his father, Lewis McDonald Grizzard, Sr., who died on August 12, 1970, at the age of fifty-six.*

Lewis, Jr., was twenty-three years old at the time, and his submerged grief is expressed powerfully in this account:

I had vowed not to cry. This was another test of my manhood, another in a series of tests I was constantly giving myself for no other reason than to prove my manhood in daddy's sight. To cry now would be a sign of my weakness. To cry now would be to disavow my adulthood. I stood there alone with my dying father. There was no mother to turn to and bury my face against for comfort. This was mine.

He continued to struggle for each breath. I thought each he took would be his last, but after a grueling pause, there would be another. The blue in his face was deepening.

The silence is deafening at a death watch. I wanted some great and furious words to say. But none came. The three men [from his church] were also silent. They obviously felt to speak and interrupt my grief would have been terribly out of place.

The last breath came. We all saw it and heard it. There was a sense of relieved sigh to it. Or maybe there wasn't. Maybe that was my imagination.

Seconds passed. Then, a minute was gone. I put my daddy's hand in mine. I held it tightly. Another minute passed. I would not speak. I knew I would not speak. Someone else would have to signal the end.

"I believe your daddy has passed," one of the men said.

I closed my eyes and held his hand. One of the men slipped out of the room. He came back with the nurse.

She took daddy's other hand and checked for a pulse. She looked up at me and found my eyes. She said nothing to me, but her eyes were the messenger. . . .

. . . I stood over the body, with daddy's hand still in mine. I was dazed. I thought of trumpets. I wanted trumpets, . . . I wanted the pealing of bells. I wanted something more than the silence. The helplessness I felt became intense. This is it, I thought. It is over and it had been so quiet, so lacking of drama. He breathed and then he didn't breathe anymore, and the nurses came and the doctor came and they pulled a sheet over his head and a man said a prayer. That had been it.

After a time, probably seconds, maybe an hour, I let daddy's hand drop beside him.

My Daddy Was a Pistol and I'm a Son of a Gun, 266–268.

Frederick Buechner, *a Presbyterian minister, is the author of ten novels and ten theological books. His father, Carl Frederick, committed suicide in the fall of 1936.*

Frederick was only ten years old at the time. . . .

On a Saturday in late fall, my brother and I woke up around sunrise. I was ten and he was not quite eight, and once we were awake, there was no going back to sleep. . . . Our mother and father were going to take us to a football game, and although we were not particularly interested in the game, we were desperately interested in being taken. . . . It was much too early to get up. . ., so we amused ourselves as best we could until the rest of the house got moving. . . .

. . . our bedroom door opened a little, and somebody looked in on us. It was our father. Later on we could not remember anything more about it than that, even when we finally got around to pooling our memories of it, which was not until many years later.

If he said anything to us, or if we said anything to him, we neither of us have ever been able to remember it. He could have been either dressed or still in his pajamas for all we noticed. There was apparently nothing about his appearance or about what he said or did that made us look twice at him. There was nothing to suggest that he opened the door for any reason other than just to check on us as he passed by on his way to the bathroom or wherever else we might have thought he was going that early on a Saturday morning. . . . I have no idea of how long he stood there looking at us. A few seconds? A few minutes? Did he smile, make a face, wave his hand? I have no idea. All I know is that after a while, he disappeared, closing the door behind him, and we went on playing. . . .

. . . How long it was from the moment he closed that door to the moment we opened it, I can no longer have any way of knowing. . . . That moment was also the last of my childhood because, when I opened the door again, measurable time was, among other things, what I opened it on.

Down below was the gravel drive, the garage with its doors flung wide open and the same blue haze thick inside it and drifting out into the crisp autumn day. I had the sense that my brother and I were looking down from a height many times greater than just the height of the second story of our house. In gray slacks and a maroon sweater, our father was lying in the driveway on his back.

The Sacred Journey, 37–40.

Clifford Arthur Koons had a stroke while driving across Los Angeles to the Azusa Pacific University campus. Carolyn was later surprised when her brother, also named Clifford, called her.

"I've got news for you." His voice changed, and I sensed him groping for words, so I waited.

"Dad died last night."

"What?"

His words shot right through me. Somehow without really thinking through it, I had always imagined my dad would outlive me.

"The hospital called last night. He died of alcoholic poisoning."

There was silence over the phone lines as the pronouncement sank in. I didn't feel anything at all. He'd been there—violent and

mean—every single day of my life. How could he and his threat just
disappear, vanish like that? Finally the silence seemed too long, and
I wanted to clear the confusion in my spirit. "Clifford, what do you
feel?" I asked softly.

With a sigh he gathered his thoughts. "Nothing."

"Neither do I," I admitted. A whole life lived, millions of words
and emotions communicated, pain and destruction strewn all along
the way, and at the end all we who knew him could feel was nothing?

Tim Hansel *is the founder and president of Summit Expeditions, a
wilderness training program, and an author. His father, Art Hansel, died
on May 2, 1985, at the age of seventy-seven.*

Tim was forty-four years old at the time. . . .

The phone call was from home. "They're taking Dad into the
hospital again. Maybe for the last time."

His long battle with cancer was nearly over.

"How's he taking it, Mom?"

"Oh, you know him. He's still chipper. I'll give you a call tonight
to let you know how he's doing. And if something happens, you know
as well as I do how incredibly blessed we've been. He's already fooled
the doctors for over three years."

I knew it well. The year before we had all prayed that Dad would
live long enough to see my *What Kids Need Most in a Dad* come out,
since it was in a very real way a tribute to him. I was hoping he would
be able to see this book, too, but it seemed he had an earlier deadline
to meet than I did.

I hung up the phone and thought about a line from a poem I'd
read recently—"God is fitting you with a whole new pair of dancing
shoes." And I sat down and wrote a few lines to my dad.

*Get your dancin' shoes ready, Pop. That's what you and Mom have
always been good at, no matter what the circumstances. You gotta keep
dancin', Pop. I'm counting on you.*

Listen to the powerful way Tim announces his father's death.

At five-fifty A.M. on May 2, 1985, Art Hansel put on his new dancin' shoes, just one week before this book was finished. My mom, my brother Steve, and I were all there for the final family reunion and were all with my father when he passed away.

He died the same way he lived, quietly and gracefully. He was a magnificent person, and though a man of few words, he echoed with his entire life what this book has been trying to say.

"Hey. . .I love you, Pop! And I'm gonna miss you, too.

"Keep those dancin' shoes handy, because when I come I'll bring mine, too—and we'll celebrate all that God has done for us.

"See ya soon, Pop."

In my copy of Tim's book, I wrote in one word: "Wow!"
You Gotta Keep Dancin', 149–150.

Moments of Comfort

Quotations Worth Remembering: The Passing

My dad cried when I told him that in heaven he would never die again. Death isn't the worst thing in life, but dying may be.

Michael Ladra

You never stop loving your daddy.

Lewis Grizzard

Someone once told me, "Your mother can have many husbands, but you can have only one father."

Peggy Griffiths

Life will never be again what it has been all these years with him behind us.

Phillips Brooks

There has never been anybody like papa.

Thomas Wolfe

Death is not the end of hope, but the beginning!

Glenn Scott Morris

Death is not the enemy we generally assume it is. Consider only the alternative: life without death. Life without death would be interminable—both literally and figuratively.

Death cannot be the enemy if it is death that brings us to life. Put differently: just as without leavetaking there can be no arrival; just as without a growing old, there can be no growing up; just as without tears, no laughter; so without death, there could be no living.

William Sloan Coffin

. . . if it were not for the certainty that he is not dead but gone before, I should perish.

Theodore Roosevelt

If I had known that that last time we were together would be the last time I would ever see you, I would have looked at you more closely. I would have listened more carefully to what you had to say. I would have said to you all the things I ever wanted to tell you.

Anonymous

When he left us, it was as if a great tree had fallen in the forest, and left a lonesome place against the sky.

Anonymous

George Buttrick once said that life is essentially a series of events to be borne and lived through, rather than a series of intellectual riddles to be played with and solved. It is important that you remember his words at a time like this. Time and time again you will ask the question, "Why has this happened?" In all probability no answer will come. The heavens will seem as brass. The silence of God will be deafening.

It is just as well! Even if an answer came, it would not satisfy. Answers do not heal broken hearts. They do not soothe the ache and loneliness that we feel in the hour of death. God is in the business of sustaining, not explaining. He has never promised to tell us why things happen.

BUT he has promised to go with us through those experiences and enable us to be victorious over them. If you stay close to him, you will discover that it is enough.

Paul Powell

What is death?

Death is the golden chariot sent by the King to fetch Cinderella.

Peter Kreeft

This is what happened to your loved one. No matter the circumstances of the death, the event itself was the pleasant passage to a new adventure.

Doug Manning

Remember St. Teresa's bold saying that from heaven the most miserable earthly life will look like one bad night in an inconvenient hotel!

Peter Kreeft

In heaven those who were handicapped on earth are the great athletes, intellectuals, or beauty queens.

Peter Kreeft

We do not know the "Whys," and the "Wheres,"
The "Whens," the "Ifs," and "Ands";
But this we know, God is wise,

For He has studied out the plans.
He, and only He, knows best—
It is He who holds the key;
And if we only stand the test
He will unlock the chains and set us free.
So, when we say, "Thy will be done,"
We must be submissive to His will;
And bow to Him, no matter how the course is run—
He will all our needs fulfill.
We do not need to say "Good bye,"
For life is such a narrow span.
We shall meet our loved ones by and by—
Then, and only then, we'll understand.

Ruth M. Clifton

We sometimes congratulate ourselves at the moment of waking from a troubled dream; it may be so the moment after death.

Nathaniel Hawthorne

What we know about you gives us the strength for what we do not know about the future. . . . We choose to believe that God is in control.

John Bowling

A good man being asked during his last illness whether he thought himself dying, "Really friend, I care not whether I am or not; for if I die I shall be with God; if I live, He will be with me."

Anonymous

Not by lamentations and mournful chants ought we to celebrate the funeral of a good man, but by hymns, for in ceasing to be numbered with mortals he enters upon the heritage of a diviner life.

Plutarch

Death and love are the two wings that bear the good man to heaven.

Michelangelo

I believe that it is not dying that people are afraid of. Something else, something more unsettling and more tragic than dying frightens us. We are afraid of never having lived, of coming to the end of our days with the sense that we were never really alive, that we never figured out what life was for.

Harold S. Kushner

Scriptures That Comfort

The Lord understands my grief.

As a father pities his children,
So the LORD pities those who fear Him.
   Ps. 103:13

My dad is not dead, he is with the Lord

And Enoch walked with God; and he was not, for
God took him.
   Gen. 5:24

He shall call upon Me, and I will answer him;
I will be with him in trouble;
I will deliver him and honor him.
With long life I will satisfy him,
And show him My salvation.
   Ps. 91:15–16

My dad's death was noticed by God.

Precious in the sight of the LORD
Is the death of his saints.
   Ps. 116:15

But what about my prayers for Dad to live?

He asked life from You, and You gave it to him—
Length of days forever and ever.
> *Ps. 21:4*

I am in the valley of death's shadow.

The LORD is my shepherd;
I shall not want.
He makes me to lie down in green pastures;
He leads me beside the still waters.
He restores my soul;
He leads me in the paths of righteousness
For His name's sake.
Yea, though I walk through the valley of the shadow
of death,
I will fear no evil;
For You are with me.
> *Ps. 23:1–4c*

Whom do I have to turn to in this time but the Lord?

Hear, O LORD, when I cry with my voice!
Have mercy also upon me, and answer me.
When you said, "Seek My face,"
My heart said to You, "Your face, LORD, I will seek."
Do not hide Your face from me;
Do not turn Your servant away in anger;
You have been my help;
Do not leave me nor forsake me,
O God of my salvation.
When my father and my mother forsake me,
Then the LORD will take care of me.
> *Ps. 27:7–10*

Jesus understands our agony at this time.

For we do not have a High Priest who cannot sympathize with our weaknesses, but was in all points tempted as we are, yet without sin. Let us therefore come boldly to the throne of grace, that we may obtain mercy and find grace to help in time of need.

Heb. 4:15–16

God gives eternal life

And this is the testimony; that God has given us eternal life, and this life is in His Son. He who has the Son has life.

1 John 5:11–12a

Jesus said. . ., "I am the resurrection and the life. He who believes in Me, though he may die, he shall live. And whoever lives and believes in Me shall die. Do you believe this?"

John 11:25–26

Blessed are the dead who die in the Lord.

Rev. 14:13

A Hymn That Comforts
Abide with Me

Abide with me! Fast falls the eventide.
The darkness deepens; Lord, with me abide.
When other helpers foil and comforts flee,
Help of the helpless, O abide with me!

Swift to its close ebbs out life's little day.
Earth's joys grow dim; its glories pass away.
Change and decay in all around I see;
O Thou who changest not, abide with me.

I need Thy presence every passing hour;
What but Thy grace can foil the tempter's power?
Who, like Thyself, my guide and stay can be?
Thro' cloud and sunshine, Lord, abide with me!

I fear no foe, with Thee at hand to bless;
Ills have no weight, and tears no bitterness.
Where is death's sting? Where, grave, thy victory?
I triumph still if Thou abide with me.

Hold Thou Thy cross before my closing eyes;
Shine thro' the gloom, and point me to the skies.
Heav'n's morning breaks, and earth's vain shadows flee!
In life, in death, O Lord, abide with me.

Henry F. Lyte, Worship in Song, *49.*

Prayers That Comfort
A prayer when death has been swift.

Gracious Lord, who loveth ail men, give us grace to be thankful
to thee for having called this thy servant home to thee, knowing that
thou hast spared him much suffering and us much sorrow, and in full
assurance that thou art doing for him better things than we can either
understand or ask for. Through Jesus Christ our Lord. *Amen.*

Geffin, *Handbook of Public Prayers,* 188.

A prayer after the suffering has ended.

Father, we come into your presence, broken by Dad's passing. It
is finally over. He has laid down the burden and picked up his crown.
All his life he said that he aimed to make heaven his home. Now, he
has done that.

I thank you for your faithfulness to him throughout the long season called suffering.

Now, I thank you for the years you gave him to us. For his presence, his life. I thank you that he was not snatched away from me when I was young; that I as an adult have had a chance to know him. I thank you that he was not snatched out in some senseless accident.

I do not understand why he suffered so much. But I am thankful that he never felt forsaken or abandoned by you.

You have urged me to cast all my care on you. So I do. Give me courage to face the responsibilities of the funeral and next few days. *Amen.*

Prayer at the death of a parent.

Father, I have so much to be thankful for today. My father lived long enough for me to know him. Strengthen me now for the responsibility that I inherit today. If in your Providence, I am ever entrusted with a high and honorable title of parenthood, may I so live that I may be an unfailing source of wisdom, security, and encouragement to my children.

Remove the guilt of my grief today. From this loss, I find that I could and should have done more. But I am not perfect. You know this, and my father knew this. I thank you for flooding this moment of my life with divine forgiveness. You are righting every wrong, and I thank you.

As the fruit of the love of my father and mother, I shall live on. I dedicate and commit myself to live honorably and respectfully so that the remainder of my years brings no disgrace to my family's name. I rejoice and thank you for Christ's promise of eternal life. "He who lives and believes in me shall never die."

"In my Father's house are many mansions."

I am strengthened by your word: "When my father and mother forsake me, then the Lord will take me up." I know that sorrow never leaves us where it finds us. I remember it is not what happens to me in life but how I react to what happens to me that is supremely important.

Now, God, you will be constantly my heavenly parent. "Weeping may endure for the night, but joy comes in the morning." *Amen*

Schuller, *Prayers*, 66–67.

THE BURYING

If a man cannot turn to god in the hour of his greatest need and come boldly to the throne of grace for help in such a time, then the gospel means nothing and christian experience is a delusion.

Vance Havner

His Obituary

"THERE IT IS!" my mother said, holding the morning newspaper in her hand, as she quickly read it again, though she already knew what it said. Three paragraphs in the *Courier-Journal* made it official: she was a widow and I was an orphaned adult. This told her that he was dead. The paper said so.

My folks always read the obituaries and compared notes. They never could tell when someone who had been a neighbor in 1936 or 1946 or 1976 might have died. You know how people lose track of each other these days. Well, the obituary column is the bulletin board for lost relationships.

Several people at the visitation said, "I saw it in the paper."

First time in his life that my father got his name in the newspaper, and he had to die to do it. Considering all the ways people get their names in the newspaper these days, it could have been worse.

It reminds me of the story I heard of the funeral of Isabel Coleman, a long-time missionary to China. At her funeral, a Chinese man stood and read her history of missionary service. In English, he concluded, "For those who did not know Miss Coleman, no words are adequate to describe her life. For those who knew her, no words are necessary" (Paul Powell, *Gospel from the Graveside*, 62).

The same is true with my dad. The obituary in the *Courier-Journal* was a bow to tradition.

The Longest Walk I Will Ever Make

I believe the longest walk I will ever make is from the front door of the funeral home to that space—that particular space—in front of the casket where I'm supposed to stand. It doesn't really matter how many other times I've stood at that spot for aunts, uncles, grandparents, friends. This time is different.

It's my dad lying there. I notice his name spelled out in the little white letters on the signboard outside the parlor.

I had seen him stretched out on the couch, napping, and he had looked similar (only he wasn't all dressed up). And he'd wake up, sometimes sheepishly, and find me.

"Been here long?" he'd ask Or, "What time is it?" Sometimes, he would offer an explanation. Or an excuse. And he'd wonder if I was buying it. It seemed slightly un-American to have my dad sleeping on the couch in the middle of the afternoon.

And some of those excuses were good. I would smile; he'd smile. But my mom would have none of it: "Dozed off, my eye! You've been asleep for an hour."

That conversation won't happen again.

Friends

I was surprised, genuinely surprised, by all the people who came to the funeral home: friends, neighbors, acquaintances, business colleagues, church folk, fellow sufferers of kidney disease. A stream of people. How could one man have known so many people? After all, at his age, a lot of people he had known and worked with had already died.

I'll never forget his neighbor, Mr. Fred Gibson, Sr., ninety years old, standing there, wiping away tears.

"Your daddy. . . ." his voice quivered. He fought for control, for Mr. Fred Gibson, Sr., was from the old school on manly emotions. "Your daddy was like a brother to me. I've. . ." He hesitated, looking away, bent over in soul pain, "lost a brother."

At some point in the thirty-five years on the block, my dad and Mr. Fred Gibson, Sr., had stopped being neighbors and had become brothers.

"Your daddy always saw things as they were. Straight-shooter, your daddy."

I don't think that Mr. Fred Gibson, Sr., was implying that I didn't shoot straight or that anyone else in particular didn't shoot straight.

Mr. Fred Gibson, Sr., was merely observing that my dad had belonged to a generation that spoke its mind. That was concerned. At some point, Mr. Fred Gibson, Sr., had learned that if my father said he'd be there to help you, he'd be there. His yes meant yes. His no meant no. I don't remember a "well. . ." being part of Dad's vocabulary. When a neighbor asked for a favor, even if it inconvenienced my father or us, he said yes.

No wonder so many folks showed up.

Some People

You need to know, if you haven't already discovered, that there are some people, some friends, who won't say anything about your father's death. And it will annoy you, perhaps anger you that your dad's death meant so little to them. Not a word beyond a mumbled, "Sorry to hear about your father."

How generic of them. Some of them can't even say the *d* word, *death!*

Sadly, some will surprise you. Because although you've talked for hours about every other topic under the sun, you get nothing out of them on this one. You may have counted on them to listen. To understand. To comfort.

Every son or daughter who has lost a father has at least one "unexplainable" friend who surprisingly says nothing. Or quickly comments, "I don't know what to say."

But, on the other hand, some people will be "there" for you. They will listen all the way to the end of the sentence. And if you repeat yourself, they won't mind. And if you break down, they will hand you a Kleenex or a hankie without a hint of embarrassment.

And long after the funeral you will remember some people.

Funeral Recollections

Funerals are an integral part of the process of saying good-bye. In many families, traditions developed across the generations dictate how the funeral will be celebrated and, in turn, impact how the funeral will be remembered.

In this section, meet again some of the sons and daughters of the last section and walk through their dad's funeral. Harry Petrakis explains that not only do friends come to pay their respects, but sometimes enemies do as well.

For three days my father's body, attired in the gilded colorful robes of his vestments, lay in state in a casket sealed under glass. For three days several thousand people passed through the catacombs, the damp basement of the church. . . . Many of them were parishioners whose confessions he had heard for more than a quarter of a century, whose sons and daughters he had married, whose grandchildren he had baptized, and over whose dead he had spoken final words. He had often shared the dark burden of their despair, and they came now in solemn, grieving lines to offer him their solace and support.

But some of the "enemies" came too:

And like an awed and silent menagerie, the man without love in him, the parrot, the duck, the monkey, the weasel, and the nanny-goat took turns standing about his bier. I was swept with bitterness and fury at the sight of them, driving them away. I remained silent during those long days because I realized that if my father had made his peace with life, I had no sanction to carry hatred over into his death.

Reflections, 93.

Many fathers have served in the armed services and have military funerals. While that adds a rich reminder of heroism, it can make the grieving more difficult, as Lewis Grizzard *explains.*

The men from the VFW lined up behind the casket. They wore their VFW caps. When the preacher had finished his final prayer, two of the men from the VFW walked to the casket and folded the flag. One of them handed it to me.

That was when I finally lost it. I held that flag in my hands, and the significance of it tore me in half. I buried my face in it and I cried hard and long. My wife put her arms around me.

I couldn't stop the sobbing. I felt the anger and the sadness and the frustration all at once. I was angry that I felt so alone in this. Why weren't the others feeling the pain I felt? Why did they seem much less cognizant of this man's worth than I was?

And God, the sadness here. And in a tiny church yard, he goes to rest beside his mother, who loved him so much, as his son cried his heart out.

I couldn't make anybody understand all this. I didn't have the words, the power to explain it. The frustration was that this was the end.

My Daddy Was a Pistol and I'm a Son of a Gun, 276–277.

The United States has made incredible progress in civil rights. Yet there are lasting reminders of racial bias and discrimination. A father's final resting place can be a lasting and painful reminder of racial injustice.

Roger Wilkins, former assistant attorney general of the United States and a Pulitzer Prize–winning journalist, recounted his father's death in 1941 at age thirty-six.

Roger was nine. . .

Three weeks after the 1940 Christmas, which was the best one I ever had, my father died at home, early in the morning, while I was still asleep. I heard a family friend tell somebody on the phone, "No, he didn't make it," and that's the way I learned that my father was dead.

On the day of the funeral, my Uncle Roy was there from New York. I was glad to see him. He was the tallest man I knew. My grandfather too was there and we were all in my room waiting for the funeral that was being arranged in the dining room down below. I was on my knees reading the funnies spread out on my bed when I heard a strange noise. I turned around and saw it was my grandfather trying to stifle his crying and my uncle trying to give comfort. My grandfather talked about how much he had loved my father, and I remembered how much my father resented him because he had given up parental responsibility when the children were young and then claimed credit for them when they grew up.

At the funeral somebody read my father's favorite poem, "Thanatopsis," and some other people said some other words and some songs were sung. Then Momma and Uncle Roy and Grandpa and the rest of us had to take him out to a segregated cemetery . . . and put him in the ground with the rest of the colored people. According to the custom of the day, he wasn't good enough to be dead with white folks.

A Man's Life: An Autobiography, 19–20.

Rocky Graziano's father, Nick Barbella, died in May 1954. Rocky was thirty-one years old. The morning of the funeral was rainy. A family who had known a great deal of tension gathered to say good-bye to their father. One expects the heavyweight boxing champion of the world to be strong. How does he handle his father's funeral?

I never got up the nerve to tell him I understood how he must have felt before I was born, how it was to give up his last hope of the big time and a good life, and turn his back on the ring. I was sorry he wasn't lucky, like I was lucky, and I should have told Pop but I never did. . . .

. . . In the church I took my mother's arm and we followed the brown casket down the aisle. Behind us came Yolanda and Dominick, and Joe and Lennie and their wives, and Ida and her husband. This is what it took after all the years and the fights and the lonesome nights and the hungry days to bring us together.

I stood, I sat, I knelt, I stood again while the three priests chanted the Requiem Mass. The old Latin words that droned out of the incense took me back to my first scared day in the Protectory, then further back to my day of confirmation in the East Side church when I wore the new blue suit and everybody said how handsome was the little redhead Rocky Bob. The priests chanted, and I looked over my mother's head to where the casket rested in the aisle.

"Good-bye, Pop," I said. "Good-bye. Forgive me, my father," I said, "and forgive me, Father of us all."

The bell rang and we stood and followed the casket out of the church into the rain. Fighting Nick Bob was going to his rest.

Somebody up There Likes Me—the Story of My Life So Far, 368–369.

Sometimes fathers have special wishes for their funerals. Sons and daughters feel obligated to fulfill those wishes because they have "promised." Consider a young Texas congressman, Lyndon Johnson. *His father, Sam Ealy Johnson, Jr., had requested that his body be carried to the grave, not in a hearse, but in an old-fashioned glass coach pulled by spirited horses. Through his political connections Lyndon found such a coach.*

The future president was twenty-nine years old when his father died.

The funeral turned out to be quite a media event for the young congressman. The governor attended and the secretary of state, having believed what Johnson had told them so many times—that his father was only an impoverished drunk—and thought they were doing Congressman Johnson a favor since so few people would attend a drunk's funeral. They were stunned to find so many people there: including veterans in both World War I and Civil War uniforms, as well as a few of Teddy Roosevelt's Rough Riders.

Robert Caro, Lyndon Johnson's biographer, describes what took place after the funeral.

A moment of tension occurred after the service when Sam's immediate family, alone in the Johnson home, was sitting around the dining-room table with Lyndon, in his father's chair, disposing of his father's personal possessions. Lyndon's three sisters and his brother, Sam Houston Johnson, had said hardly a word, but when Lyndon reached out and started to take the watch for himself, Lucia, the youngest and the meekest of the sisters, put her hand on his arm and stopped him. "No," she said. "You can't have the watch. That belongs to Houston now. Daddy wanted him to have it. We all know that." Rebekkah took the watch and handed it to Lyndon's younger brother.

Sam Houston Johnson was to write: "It was an embarrassing moment for Lyndon, and I felt sorry for him. As a matter of fact, I wanted him to have it because he was the oldest brother—but I didn't press the point for fear of antagonizing my sisters."

So Lyndon did not inherit the watch or much of anything, for that matter. He went into debt to pay for a funeral befitting the father of a United States congressman. But his biographer, Robert Caro, says he did inherit the family fear that the Johnson men had weak hearts and died young.

Lyndon Johnson became deeply depressed, and it lasted for months. Twice, in a few months, he was hospitalized for bronchitis, pneumonia, and nervous exhaustion. Political buddies tried to cheer him up by talking of his future and a career under Mr. Sam Rayburn in the House of Representatives, to which he replied, "Too slow. Too slow."

Then in 1939, Lyndon's Uncle George died at age fifty-seven of "a massive heart attack." Lyndon now had no time to waste.

Twenty-one years later, Lyndon Johnson, majority leader of the US Senate, was a leading contender for the Democratic presidential nomination. On Christmas morning 1958, "Sam Houston [Johnson] wrapped the watch and gave it to Lyndon. He recalls telling his brother: 'I want you to have it. Daddy really wanted you to have it. Anyway, I'm liable to leave it somewhere.'"

Caro, *The Years of Lyndon Johnson: The Path to Power,* 542–544.

Natan Sharansky *had received a Book of Psalms the day after his thirty-second birthday. Since prisoners were forbidden to have reading materials that had been printed abroad (the book was published in Israel and written in Hebrew), the book had been confiscated.*

Just before Natan learned of his father's death, the book was returned to him somewhat mysteriously. Those Psalms became a part of his grieving process. . . .

I didn't want to do anything on the day I received the telegram [informing Natan of his father's death], not on the following day, but then I remembered the Psalm book. I opened it and immediately decided that I must read all 150 of the Psalms—not sometime in the future, but starting today.

The print was very tiny and my eyes began to hurt as soon as I looked at the text. Ignoring the pain, I began to copy the Psalms in large letters onto a sheet of paper, which took at least an hour for each one. After giving my eyes a long rest, I began translating. . . .

I can't say that I understood the Psalms completely, but I sensed their spirit and felt both the joy and the suffering of King David, their author. His words lifted me above the mundane and directed me toward the Eternal. I especially liked Psalm 23. . . .

Following the Jewish custom of mourning, I refused to shave, and the guards did not insist on it. The guard in charge of shaving and haircuts, a malicious Tatar, showed an unexpected respect for an alien tradition, a tradition about which I knew only slightly more than he did.

For forty days I copied the Psalms and read them. For one thing, it was intense work, which left me almost no time for sad thoughts and painful recollections. . . . Day after day I reconciled myself with the past, and my feelings of grief and loss were gradually replaced by sweet sorrow and fond hopes.

Although I could not visit my father's grave, I knew I would think of him whenever I came across these marvelous Psalms. They were a memorial in my heart that would stay with me forever.

A few months later Mama wrote to seek my advice about the inscription on Papa's gravestone. Not surprisingly, I turned to the Psalms—in particular, to Psalm 25, with its prophetic reference to Israel, to my father, and to his imprisoned but hopeful son. The verse read, "His soul will rest in peace, for his seed shall inherit the Land."

Fear No Evil, 272–273.

Moments of Comfort

Quotations Worth Remembering: The Burying

Men fear death, as children fear to go into the dark; and as that natural fear in children is increased with tales, so is the other.

Francis Bacon

So he passed over and the trumpets sounded
For him on the other side.

John Bunyan, Pilgrim's Progress

Timor mortis mortee pejor.
The fear of death is worse than death.

Richard Burton, Anatomy of Melancholy

So that he seemed to depart not from life, but from one home to another.

Cornelius Nepos, Atticus

Death is the golden key that opens the palace of eternity.

John Milton

Death is not a foe, but an inevitable adventure.

Sir Oliver Dodge

We call it death to leave this world, but were we once out of it, and instated into the happiness of the next, we should think it were dying indeed to come back to it again.

Sherlock

Death is not, to the Christian, what it has often been called, "Paying the debt of nature." No, it is not paying a debt; it is rather like bringing a note to a bank to obtain solid gold in exchange for it. You bring a cumbrous body which is nothing worth, and which you could not wish to retain long; you lay it down, and receive for it, from the eternal treasures, liberty, victory, knowledge and rapture.

John Foster

My five-year-old son, Twig, was there at the service for his grandfather that beautiful spring day. Twig and I have often sat down together to talk since then. We have talked about death, about his grandfather, and about God. Nina too often talks of her Opa [grandfather], and as she grows older she will fashion her own questions about death and God. As for now, she simply says that when she grows up she wants to be God, because God never dies.

F. Forrester Church

They say that an infant is born with a clenched fist, but a man dies with an open hand. Life has a way of prying loose our grasp on all that seems so important.

J. V. Morsch

It is difficult to assess any personality; when that personality is one's father the image is clouded by many things: love, proximity, youthful impressions, and that splendid "taken for granted" attitude with which children eye their parents.

Ruth Leslie Howard

Nothing of God dies when a man of God dies.

A W. Tozer

One short sleep past, we wake eternally,
And Death shall be no more;
Death, thou shall die.

John Donne, Divine Poems

We understand death for the first time when he puts his hand upon
one whom we love.

Madame de Staël

Not lost, but gone before.

Matthew Henry,
from *Commentaries: Matthew 2*

Behold—not him we knew!
This was the prison which his soul looked through.

Oliver Holmes,
from *The Last Look*

There is no death! The stars go down
To rise upon some other shore
And bright in Heaven's jeweled crown
They shine for ever more.

John L. McCreery

Death is but a path that must be trod,
If man would ever pass to God.

Thomas Parnell, A Night Piece on Death

This world is the land of the dying;
The next is the land of the living.

Tryon Edwards

Let nothing disturb thee
Let nothing dismay thee
All things pass:
God never changes.
Patience attains
All that it strives for.
He who has God
Finds he lacks nothing
God alone suffices.

St. Theresa of Avila

I know of but one remedy against the fear of death that is effectual and that will stand the test either of a sickbed, or a sound mind— that is, a good life, a clear conscience, an honest heart, and a well-ordered conversation; to carry the thoughts of dying men about us, and so to live before we die as we shall wish we had when we come to it.

Henry Ward Beecher

By and by you will hear people say, "Mr. Moody is dead!" Don't believe a word of it. At that very moment, I shall be more alive than I am now. I shall *then* begin to live.

D. L. Moody

Scriptures That Comfort
Jesus' words of assurance for a funeral.

"Let not your heart be troubled; you believe in God, believe also in Me. In My Father's house are many mansions; if it were not so, I would have told you. I go to prepare a place for you. And if I go and prepare a place for you, I will come again and receive you to Myself; that where I am, there you may be also. And where I go you know, and the way you know."

Thomas said to Him, "Lord, we do not know where You are going, and how can we know the way?"

Jesus said to him, "I am the way, the truth, and the life. No one comes to the Father except through Me."

John 14:1–6

A funeral is a time to trust

For I know that my Redeemer lives,
And He shall stand at last on the earth;
And after my skin is destroyed,
  this I know,
That in my flesh I shall see God,
Whom I shall see for myself,
And my eyes shall behold,
  and not another.
How my heart yearns within me!

Job 19:25–27

Death is a mystery.

Behold, I tell you a mystery: We shall not all sleep, but we shall all be changed—in a moment, in the twinkling of an eye, at the last trumpet. For the trumpet will sound, and the dead will be raised incorruptible, and we shall be changed.

1 Cor. 15:51–52

Then shall be brought to pass the saying that is written: "Death is swallowed up in victory."

O Death, where is your sting?
O Hades, where is your victory?

1 Cor. 15:54–55

The promise of tears.

Those who sow in tears
Shall reap in joy.
He who continually goes forth weeping,
Bearing seed for sowing,
Shall doubtless come again with rejoicing,
Bringing his sheaves with him.
   Ps. 126:5–6

Look up for help.

I will lift up my eyes to the hills—
From whence comes my help?
My help comes from the Lord,
Who made heaven and earth.
He will not allow your foot to be moved;
He who keeps you will not slumber.
Behold, He who keeps Israel
Shall neither slumber nor sleep.
The LORD is your keeper;
The LORD is your shade at your right hand.
The sun shall not strike you by day,
Nor the moon by night.
The LORD shall preserve you from all evil;
He shall preserve your soul.
The LORD shall preserve your going out and your
coming in
From this time forth, and even forevermore.
   Ps. 121

God will hear you during this time of loss.

I called on the LORD in distress;
The LORD answered me and set me in a broad place.

The LORD is on my side;
I will not fear.
Ps. 118:5–6

The pains of death encompassed me,
And the pangs of Sheol laid hold of me;
I found trouble and sorrow.
Then I called upon the name of the LORD:
"O LORD, I implore You, deliver my soul!"
I love the LORD, because He has heard
My voice and my supplications.
Because He has inclined His ear to me,
Therefore I will call upon Him as long as I live.
Ps. 116:3–4, 1–2

The LORD is near to all who call upon Him,
To all who call upon Him in truth.
He will fulfill the desire of those who fear Him;
He also will hear their cry and save them.
The LORD preserves all who love Him.
Ps. 145:18–20a

The LORD upholds all who fall,
And raises up all those who are bowed down.
Ps. 145:14

He heals the brokenhearted
And binds up their wounds.
Ps. 147:3

The LORD raises those who are bowed down;
The LORD loves the righteous.

The LORD watches over the strangers;
He relieves the fatherless and widow.
>   *Ps. 146:8–9*

Where can I go from Your Spirit?
Or where can I flee from Your presence?
If I ascend into heaven, You are there;
If I make my bed in hell, behold,
>   You are there.
If I take the wings of the morning,
And dwell in the uttermost parts of the sea,
Even there Your hand shall lead me,
And Your right hand shall hold me.
>   *Ps. 139:7–10*

A Hymn That Comforts
Under His Wings

Under his wings I am safely abiding.
Tho' the night deepens and tempests are wild,
Still I can trust Him; I know He will keep me.
He has redeemed me, and I am His child.

Under His wings, what a refuge in sorrow!
How the heart yearningly turns to His rest!
Often when earth has no balm for my healing,
There I find comfort, and there I am blest.

Under His wings, oh, what precious enjoyment!
There will I hide till life's trials are o'er;
Sheltered, protected, no evil can harm me.
Resting in Jesus, I'm safe evermore.

Under His wings, under His wings,
Who from His love can sever?
Under His wings my soul shall abide,
Safely abide forever.

William O. Cushing, Worship in Song, *451*.

Prayers That Comfort
I am somewhat hesitant to include a prayer that is so old because we rarely speak with -th endings. Remaineth *is hardly common in our vocabularies. But, it is helpful to know that three hundred years ago, people were mourning over the deaths of their fathers, too, and that they found comfort in these words.*

A prayer for strength for the burial service.

O Lord God, we remember before Thee all Thy servants who have departed this life in faith and fear, and especially him whom Thou hast now taken unto Thyself. For all Thy loving kindness to him throughout his earthly life we give Thee thanks. We bless Thee that for him all sickness and sorrow are ended, that death itself is past, and that he has entered into the rest that remaineth for Thy people, through Jesus Christ our Lord.

We beseech Thee that being inspired by the example of those who have gone before, we may run with patience the race that is set before us, looking unto Jesus, the Author and Finisher of our faith, so that when this changeful life shall have passed away we may meet with those Thou hast loved, in the Kingdom of Thy Glory, through Jesus Christ our Lord.

Father of mercies and God of all comfort, in tender love and mercy, we beseech Thee look on Thy servants who are in sorrow. Enable them to find in Thee their Refuge and Strength, and to know the love of Christ which passeth knowledge, that their faith and hope may be in Him, who by death hath taken away the sting of death, and rising again hath opened the gates of life everlasting.

Now be with us as we follow to the grave the body of our father here departed, not sorrowing as those who have no hope, but believing that as Jesus died and rose again, so them also who sleep in Jesus wilt Thou bring with *Him. Amen.*

Church of Scotland, Ordinal and Service Book.

A prayer of surrender.

Our Father, we surrender that which we loved the most into thy keeping. Let the knowledge of the reality of thy love comfort us in this hour. May heaven seem so close to us now that each thought and each act of ours may be done as in thy presence. Renew our faith as each day passes. Help us to look in hope for the time when we shall be reunited with our loved one in the kingdom of our Lord; for in his name we pray. *Amen.*

William R. and John Baird, *Funeral Meditations,* 94.

3

THE MOURNING

Grieving is as natural as crying when you are hurt, sleeping
when you are tired, eating when you are hungry, or sneezing
when your nose itches. It's nature's way of healing a broken
heart.

Doug Manning

Mausoleum

I WISH NOW he were buried at eye level because I have to look up.
Maybe that's the way it should be. A son should always look up to his
dad.

A Pain Called Guilt

I wrestle with the guilt that I had not called my dad as often as I should
have, as often as I could have. Why didn't I call?

Because I had no words to ease his pain. But now I suspect that
just my voice would have been sufficient for a man who had already
come to terms with pain.

Somehow It's Different Without a Father

People say, "Tell me about your family." It's an expected part of
American "getting-to-know-you" conversation. But in such moments
I have such a hard time saying, "My father's dead. . ." or "My father
died in October. . . ."

You'd think by now I'd be comfortable with the phrase, with the reality. You'd think by now I would have gotten used to his death. After all, I'm an adult, not a small boy who misses his father's throwing baseballs in the backyard after supper.

I so dislike that phrase *used to it.* I can't figure out a way to get used to his death. The words still stall between my heart and my throat. The words refuse to cooperate, and I stutter. I lose that edge of control.

In those moments, right in the middle of a conversation, I often want to be alone for a while with my thoughts. With my memories.

A Good Cry

If I weren't sitting in a major airport right now, I think I would have a good cry.

But society says no to that behavior. And my dad was part of that society. He taught me, "Big boys don't cry." He discounted my protests: "But, Daddy, it hurts!"

If my sister were here, she could cry, and no one would say a thing. My heartbreak is just as severe, and I am supposed to sit here and take it "like a man."

Right at this moment, I don't want to be a man. I want some relief from this ache inside. No wonder grown men have aches and pains that physicians cannot find.

Dad always said after he had punished me, "Quit crying, or I'll give you something to cry about!"

Dad, you did just that. By dying.

Then

I've always been good about tackling deadlines, getting assignments finished ahead of time. Virtues my dad taught me. But this writing has been a bear. Because I feel drained, exhausted. And there's no one to kiss it and make it all better or, at least, a little better.

My dad often said to me, "You're a big boy *now.*"

I hear those words in his voice. Although I know he is dead, it's as if I can turn around in my chair and expect to see Dad standing in the doorway.

After I left home, after I married, after I received my doctorate, when life stumped me, I could pick up the phone and call my dad. I can remember other times when things "got better" after just a few words with him.

But that was then.

My dad's death fast-forwarded me into the next generation. I am really on my own now. Death has an ugly finality.

I've got to get used to the pain and console myself with the belief, no, the conviction that someday I will see Dad again.

And some of the things that we couldn't talk about will not matter in that world. And on that day my dad will say, as he did so many times, "Welcome home, son."

For All Those Years My Dad Was There

For all those years my dad was there

- to repair bicycles,
- to patch deflated basketballs and egos,
- to chase away boogiemen,

of which there have never been a shortage, even for a grown man making mortgage payments, the interest on which would have paid the principal on my father's.

It's as if an announcement was made over some public address system wherever boogiemen hang out: "Harold Ivan Smith is now defenseless." So they all line up to have a go at me, and I sense that they have been waiting for *this* moment.

Because some of them still remember the last time when my dad ran them off and told them in no uncertain terms: "Never, Ever! Ever!!! come back, OR. . . ." And he never had to fill in the blank because then he said, in the most soothing voice a child could ever hear, "There now, go back to sleep." And I woke up the next morning barely remembering the incident.

It seems just last night that I was a child, he was alive, and I was convinced there wasn't anything my dad couldn't handle.

And now he has up and died on me.

For all those years he was there for those "What do you think?" kind of questions. Sometimes, I knew my world and his world were so different that he wouldn't have a good answer. Or any answer. Or that he might be hesitant to answer.

In fact, I suspected, at times, my dad felt a little put on the spot by being asked such a question. I knew that he worried about me—although he would have denied it. And that sometimes he didn't tell me everything that was on his mind.

Sometimes, it was his clichés—things he had said before that he would now repeat. Words that sounded so much like what I had expected him to say that they brought a hint of comfort.

"Didn't everything work out the last time? And the time before that? And the time before that?" I smiled.

"Well, then," he would say, with his own slight smile, "it will be all right *this* time."

And I believed him. Again. Because he was my dad.

Dad isn't ever going to say, "Where are you?. . . How's the weather?. . . Here's your mother." His conversational big three, anytime I called. But the toughest part is that he never answers the phone. I had gotten used to his always being the first voice I heard when I dialed that familiar number. Unless, of course, one of the grandchildren got there first.

Over these last years, it had become protocol for my dad to answer the phone. And more than once he said, "I thought it might be you." Which was as close as he would come to saying, "I hoped it was you."

His voice always told how he was feeling, even if his words said otherwise.

My Father's Sixth Sense

My father had that sixth sense when something was wrong. I couldn't fool him—even when I thought I had. Most days there was no point pretending.

When I was seven he would demand, "Tell me the truth." And at seven, I wouldn't dare to fib because I was so convinced that he could see right through me and that the truth would triumph and come out. And by that time, things would be such a big mess that only Dad could solve them.

He had that way of looking right into my soul. Not maliciously. But fatherly.

But when I was twenty-seven, he would sometimes ask a second time, "Are you sure? Nothing's wrong?"

More than once all I could get out was, "Oh, Dad. . . ." Then it was like some dam high in the soul cracked. My emotions came gushing out.

But on some days, for some reason, I looked away or mumbled, "Nothing."

I didn't fool him. He'd been my dad long enough to know "nothing" meant "something."

Days Like Today

It's days like today, when I did "good"—performed well, rang the bell, hit the target—that I would like to tell him about it.

Today was one of those crucial moments that has a long-term impact on a chosen career. An opportunity of a lifetime. The chance to speak to 6,500 people in the Nashville Convention Center.

Long ago Dad was there to encourage me when I spoke to fifty-five people in his church. He had listened to my stories about speaking to one thousand people. But this would have been something. And I would have felt more comfortable facing that audience, knowing that my father was thinking about me.

He always kept my schedule close by. Every news bulletin of a plane crash produced a moment of anxiety for him until he checked the schedule and found I was off in a different direction.

But how do I know he wasn't thinking about me today as I spoke to those 6,500 people? How do I know that God didn't pull back the drapes for a little while and let my dad watch?

Maybe that's one reason that things went well today: Dad was watching.

A Day to Remember

Today was my dad's birthday. If he had lived, he would have been seventy-seven. Ah, if he had lived. What a difference those four words make.

Now what am I to do with this day that has been so important in my family? His birthdays were not, at least in the years he was ill, loud affairs. But the day did not go unnoticed either: birthday cards and presents and kisses and calls and a cake of some sort, although he was just as happy with my mother's cobbler.

I know some people who keep track of their dad's birthday long after he has died.

I think his day of birth is no longer as important as his date of death. For in eternity, his date of death becomes his eternal birthday. And boy, do they celebrate!

That First Christmas Eve

That first Christmas Eve, I couldn't, I *wouldn't* imagine him gone. And everyone acted really brave about the whole thing. And I did fine— until I slipped away for a while and went to the mausoleum. I wanted to leave a rose.

I had not anticipated that the marble would be so cold. It didn't matter that I had been so composed at the funeral. Today, Christmas Eve, I wept like an orphan. Of course, it didn't seem appropriate to be sobbing at the grave of a man who had said, on at least a thousand occasions, "Stop crying! Or I'll give you something to cry about."

"But, Daddy," I could have convincingly argued, "I have something to cry about. It's Christmas and you aren't here and this doesn't feel like Christmas." And there had been no present to buy for him, either. He was difficult to buy for; he had everything and he wanted nothing. He wanted things money couldn't buy, like health.

Finally, after a good thorough cry, I whispered, "See you, Dad," and walked out like an actor on stage pretending it was Christmas Eve anyway.

That's the way he would have wanted it.

Following Tradition

We gathered at the usual place. We gathered at the usual time. We ate the usual food. We followed the tradition.

All the while we pretended that none of us were missing him.

Now when I think back on that first Christmas without him, I get angry.

I know someone should have said what was on all our hearts: "I miss him."

But everyone was trying to be so brave that no one had the courage to say the words that would have made us all stop a while and cry. But a good cry would have sent us out into the cold night air with a renewed spirit of gratitude for the years we had him.

His Last Christmas

July of that year, 1986, he never thought he'd see Christmas. But there he sat in the easy chair, watching the chaos his family called Christmas. Gifts everywhere. Food everywhere. People everywhere. Naturally all talking at the same time, having one big conversation and several smaller ones going at the same time. Ready to switch subjects in a second, sometimes without clear signals. Trying to do a year's worth of catching up in a few hours.

Daddy loved it.

His clan. His tribe. We always gathered on Christmas Eve. And as he watched his great-grandchildren opening gifts, I'm sure he remembered their parents—his grandchildren—opening presents. And their parents—his children—opening theirs just as excitedly. Where had the years gone?

As I watched him taking it all in, I wondered about that first Depression-era Christmas in 1932 that he and my mother spent as husband and wife, on a little farm in southern Indiana. Poor. The only things they had to exchange were some oranges. Could he have foreseen such a night fifty years later?

After things had settled down, my sister knelt on one side and I on the other. I will always treasure that conversation we had with Dad.

"I didn't think I would be here," he said, his chin trembling, little tears forming on his eyelids (big tears on ours). My sister was quick to cut short such statements; she could not bear the thought of a Christmas without him.

But in those few moments, although he was in pain, I doubt he had ever been more thankful. Not just for all the gifts four generations had given him that night. But for the time to be with all of us. The opportunity to spend one more Christmas with his family.

A Tribute to My Dad on Father's Day

Most people have to rely on the creativity of an artist and the way of a writer with words to compose an appropriate Father's Day card.

In late 1980 I doubted that my father would live to celebrate his seventieth birthday. So I wrote a tribute to him and submitted it to a magazine. The editor started to postpone it a year since he was also considering another article by me for the June 1981 issue. I called and asked him to reconsider, explaining that due to my father's precarious health. . . .

The editor ran the article. A lot of sons and daughters copied the article and included a copy in with their cards for their fathers. My dad was a little embarrassed by the attention.

He lived to enjoy seven more Father's Days. Each person who attended his memorial service received a copy as a tribute.

Father's Day will come again and Hallmark will be ready for those "who care enough to send the very best." Most of us will spend time selecting *just* the right card for our dads. In many ways, Father's Day cards are more difficult to select than Mother's Day cards because we don't want them to be too sentimental.

The kind of card we send is a testimony to our fathers. I've searched through a lot of cards; many with double entendre, sometimes barely concealed, others with references to "booze and broads."

That jarred me. What kind of son or daughter would send such a thought? I realize that not everyone has had a heaven-bound father. Some of us have taken for granted the godly influence of our fathers. So, on Father's Day we will sing "Faith of Our Fathers." And that hymn will be on hold until next year. It's too bad we sing that song only once a year, because the phrase we need to hear, *"By kindly words and virtuous life,"* must sink in. What kind of example are fathers in our contemporary scene?

Television has done a great deal to question the reliability of "old Dad." In too many series he has been seen as somewhat inept and out-of-it.

Remember that taunt from childhood days, "My dad is bigger than your dad!" To which we would retort, "O yeah, well. . . ."

Although my dad worked long hours, he always thought prayer meeting was important enough for him to be there.

Although he worked hard for his money, he thought tithing was essential. And he didn't stop with just 10 percent. His billfold was always open to the church. Occasionally, that meant closed to us, or at least not as open as we preferred.

Although my dad had a demanding job, he made time to serve the local church.

There was a period in my life when I was embarrassed because my dad was the church janitor. So he cleaned up the floor when Sheila Evans threw up just before the VBS demonstration program. He cleaned up all the hay from the Nativity scene because the pageant director thought her job was over when the applause ended.

We went early; we stayed late. The job paid only thirty dollars a month, but my dad thought it was important that the Lord's house be clean—really clean; be warm or cool, despite the weather; be attractive and neat. So, he got out of bed to shovel snow, to fire the furnace, to dust the pews, to make sure the bases were covered.

He could have said, "You only get so many hours of work for thirty dollars," but he didn't. There was always something that needed fixing or rearranging or painting or cleaning.

So, he didn't develop hobbies, fish, swim, golf, hunt, or jog—he just worked. When the new church was built, he worked forty hours on his job and forty plus on the new church site.

He couldn't deal with people who mistreated the church or allowed it to be mistreated. We quickly learned that it didn't matter what other people's kids did—there were definite expectations for the Smith kids.

One hot July night the adults were all standing in the back of the church visiting after the service. A group of us kids thought it would be neat to slide across the highly polished altar railing. That broke my dad's heart, because in his view the altar was for seekers' noses rather than little boys' bottoms.

In what seemed like "the twinkling of an eye" my brother and I were transported to the boiler room for moments of interaction. Since that night there has never been a hint of temptation to slide across an altar railing.

My dad is now retired; younger men run things now, both where he worked and where he worships. His health has failed. I guess I think God should have rewarded him with good health in retirement for all the years he worked so hard. But life's not like that.

I've thought he was too "old-fashioned," too rigid, too tough. I haven't always agreed with his politics or policies. But I have yet to hear him tell an off-color joke, rate a woman's figure in suggestive terms or gestures; brag about hedging on his income tax or taking a day of "sick leave" to hunt or fish; swear, smoke, drink, or report what it cost him to send me to a Christian college.

I've never heard him complain about being my father.

So, what's he got to show for it? Well, if nothing else, a son who loves him. And on this Father's Day, there will be dads who have perhaps given more monetarily, but will receive less in return.

He'll never leave me a gold mine to inherit. But he has given me a living endowment of a godly heritage and a model of faithfulness.

What more could a son have needed?

"A Tribute to Dad," *Herald of Holiness,* 5–6.

Father's Day

Today is Father's Day. Hallmark and all the calendars say it's so. My heart disagrees. I know all about the tradition of wearing a red carnation if your father is living and a white carnation if he is deceased.

This is my first Father's Day without Dad. I never thought it would feel like this. Just picking between two boutonnieres has reminded me of my loss.

There was no present to select.

There was no phone call to make to wish a happy day.

There was no celebration.

For me, Father's Day was another reminder of how soon we forget. The world has gone right on celebrating, in spite of the fragile condition of my heart this third Sunday in June.

The words of Ebenezer Scrooge come to mind: "I will keep Christmas in my heart."

Maybe that is wise advice for Father's Day as well: I will keep Father's Day *in my heart.*

We Were Different

I still remember that hot August night in 1968 when the cops were bashing college kids' heads outside the Democratic National Convention in Chicago.

Dad and I sat there, watching the chaos on TV. Two generations viewing the same images, the same event, so differently.

My dad thought Mayor Daley was a hero! I thought Daley was a dictator.

"He'll show 'em who's boss!" Dad thundered; then, in the same breath, he announced he was going to bed. Obviously, the mayor and his police force had everything under control. My dad could sleep without concern.

Only then was it safe for me to lose control, because I knew that if only I had had more courage I would not have been sitting on a sofa at 4809 Beech Drive. I would have been on those picket lines. With my generation. We were the ones facing Vietnam.

But I still had a year of college left, and I needed tuition money. And the guy who paid that tuition had an "America: Love It or Leave It!" bumper sticker on his heart. I have often regretted my cowardice that hot August night. But how could I have faced down a Chicago blueshirt when I couldn't even confront my dad?

Redneck

I'd be lying to you and to myself if I didn't tell you that my dad was a borderline redneck. I have never been able to admit that to myself. Oh, I have said that about other people's fathers, but never mine. I guess it's a holdover from all the "Honor thy father and mother" training.

But I have wondered if my dad voted for George Wallace back in 1972. He sure got a lot of votes from some people's fathers.

To reduce the stress between us, I pretended that I hadn't heard some of his comments (even though I had). You see, I grew to let my dad get away with his opinions. By that point I had given up trying to change them. And I decided, yes, *decided* to concentrate on loving him. Even if his neck was red, his heart was pure.

I think that deep in his memories were reasons why he saw things the way he saw them, reasons I could never appreciate because I had never experienced them.

No matter. Even redneck daddies need to have their necks hugged by their sophisticated sons and daughters. Regularly. It's good for the souls of both.

Healing

My father had such high expectations for me. He wanted for me a life that he had dreamed about. But he was not a man to display affection. He never told me that he loved me. When he lost his patience with me, he could be overbearing. There were times he whipped me when a word would have been sufficient.

And "I'm sorry" wasn't in his vocabulary.

For a long time, I held a grudge about that. I needed to hear him tell me that he loved me. He told my sister he loved her, so why couldn't he say that to me?

Well, I decided two can play that game. So I stopped telling him that I loved him. Stubbornness seemed to run in the family. Like father, like son. So both of us let years pass without using the word *love*. Oh, we shook hands formally. But he shook hands with everyone.

As his condition deteriorated and as I realized that he was old school and I was new school, I decided my father wasn't going to change. If changing was to be done, I had to do it.

If I had been assured that as soon as I said, "I love you," he would say something like, "Well, I love you too," it would have been so much easier. But he didn't. At least, not for a long time.

It took so much time, but the gap between us had been narrowed and was narrowing. I think that with a little more time, we both could have reached out and touched hands and found no gap at all.

Perhaps the narrowing we accomplished was enough of a miracle.

I'll Be Honest

I'll be honest and say that he was not the man I would have chosen to be my father had I been consulted.

We were so alike. We were so different.

Our egos always seemed to bump and bruise. Sometimes without warning.

He was never my idol. I early recognized his faults. I set up expectations he could not meet. I set up comparisons he always lost. I set up barriers he could not bridge. But he loved me anyway. And lately I have come to recognize more of his virtues. So . . . he was always and will always be my father.

Resemblance

I had never noticed before how many men looked like my dad. I see them in airports, in supermarkets. A feature—whether a cocked head or a side shot—resembles him. I've had those moments, awesome moments, when I was convinced that I saw my father.

A few months ago, while I was sitting in a Cracker Barrel restaurant in Spartanburg, South Carolina, enjoying my lunch, I stopped the fork halfway to my mouth. Just across the dining room sat a man— about the same age, same weight, same body type, hair, glasses. My meal got cold as I watched him. It was all I could do to keep from following him outside and asking him if I could hug him.

Or a year ago, driving across Kansas on Super Bowl Sunday, trying to make it home to see the kickoff. I topped a little rise and came upon an older couple out for their Sunday drive. I looked to my right as I passed them and slammed on my brakes. It scared them as much as it scared me. That man didn't kind of look like my dad. I'm talking spitting image. Clone. Twin. Double.

Then I felt so dumb for scaring them that I stepped on my accelerator and showed them my license plate. I could imagine them saying, "What in the world?"

For fifty miles, I drove in silence.

Or just the other day, when I was speaking in a church in Dallas. Ten rows back, on the left side, end of the aisle, he sat. Same glasses. Same suit. Same thinning gray hair. And I watched how he struggled to his feet when the congregation stood for prayer.

I am a professional speaker and I am supposed to be "in control" at all times. So I was. But later, when I had time to really think about it, I was uneasy. Was I losing my mind?

Recollections of Mourning

After those experiences of seeing my father, I thought I should tell someone—a friend, a counselor, or a psychologist—about what had happened. Then I decided that it would sound most unstable. Better just keep this to myself.

But as I continued to look for other sons' and daughters' experiences, I found some of them had shared this illusion. Maybe it was a normal part of my grieving for my dad.

I begin this section with two such experiences: those of Norman Vincent Peale *and* Doug Manning.

Norman Vincent Peale, the well-known author and clergyman, was preaching at a Methodist gathering in Georgia when he thought he saw his father, Charles Clifford Peale, a Methodist minister who had died in 1955 at the age of eighty-five.

Norman was fifty-seven years old at the time. . . .

During the meeting there was an inspiring song service, and my friend Bishop Arthur Moore asked all the preachers in the congregation to come to the platform, form a choir, and sing together. As they came down the aisles, they were singing with the great congregation that old hymn, "At the cross, at the cross, where I first saw the light." I was sitting on the platform, feeling relaxed and happy. Then suddenly, among the preachers coming down the center aisle, I saw my dear old father.

Before he died, my father had suffered several strokes, and his voice was reduced to a whisper. But here he came, vigorously singing, and with a wonderful light on his face; he seemed about forty; he was trim and vital and healthy and handsome, and he was smiling at me. When he raised his hand in the old familiar gesture, it was so real that I came up out of my chair and started forward to meet him. What the other people thought I don't know, but for me there were only my father and I in that big auditorium. Then, suddenly, I could see him no more, but the feeling of his presence in my heart was indisputable. I am not superstitious. I don't think I am over-excitable or hallucination-prone. I am just telling you what I saw and felt, and it was one of the realest experiences of my life. And why not? My father was a Methodist preacher. He loved the old gatherings and the old songs. I believe he was there, in spirit. It's just the sort of place he would love to be. And he would be so happy to be there with me preaching. It was all so like him, so very natural.

How was I able to see him? I don't know. We were momentarily in contact, that's all. In his book, *The Unobstructed Universe,* Steward Edward Williams suggests an analogy. He points out that when the blades of an electric fan are at rest, or slowly moving, you can't see through them. But when the fan is revolving at top speed you can see through all the points in the circle in which the blades are revolving, because they are now in a higher frequency. Is it not at least conceivable, therefore, that around us now in this mysterious universe are those we have loved and lost for a while, but that between us is a barrier through which we can see only in rare moments when for some reason the frequency in them corresponds with some higher frequency in ourselves? I think so.

The Healing of Sorrow, 41–42.

Because this experience is so new to us, particularly if a father is the first parent to die, sons and daughters may struggle with their emotions. It takes a seasoned minister who has dealt with hundreds of funerals to offer "explanations" that can comfort. Doug Manning *has that kind of experience.*

You may have had an experience in the last few weeks when it seemed as if the person was there with you. It may have been an almost physical thing when you felt the presence as real as life itself. Many people experience such an event. Most are afraid to report it because they think no one will understand. Some are even afraid they are crazy.

This experience is a fairly common occurrence; you are not crazy. There are many things we do not know about life beyond. Who can say there is not a chance for a loved one to come by just to say good-bye?

Don't Take My Grief Away, 46.

Fathers sometimes leave such personal legacies that sons and daughters despair of being able to follow. Young Theodore Roosevelt *doubted that he could ever live up to his father's expectations. His early life and career were deeply influenced not only by his father's death, but by the deaths of his mother, Martha, and his young bride, Alice, in the same house, on the same day, Valentine's Day 1884. The future president was left with a one-year-old daughter.*

When his father, also named Theodore, died in 1878 at age forty-six, the future president was twenty-one. One month later he wrote:

My father shared all my joys, and in sharing doubled them, and soothed all the few sorrows I ever had.

[My father was] the only human being to whom I told *everything,* never failing to get loving advice and sweet sympathy in return; no one, but my wife, if ever I marry, will ever be able to take his place.

O, Father, Father, how bitterly I miss you, mourn you, and long for you!

Harbaugh, *Power and Responsibility: The Life and Times of Theodore Roosevelt*, 6–7.

Many sons and daughters have not enjoyed a close relationship with their fathers. That loss can taunt them for the rest of their life. Some have been emotionally rejected by fathers. Such was the relationship between Sir Winston Churchill, *two-time prime minister of Great Britain and winner of the Nobel Peace Prize, and his father, Lord Randolph Churchill, who died in 1895 at age forty-six.*

Winston was twenty-one at the time of his father's death. One of Churchill's biographers wrote:

It was the image of his father which dominated and obsessed his being. It was in truth an image of his own creation that he worshiped. He did not know his father, nor does Lord Randolph appear to have made any attempt to know his son, whose intelligence he rated so low that he considered him unfit to practice at the Bar. . . .

The icy detachment and indifference of Lord Randolph failed to destroy the proud and passionate allegiance of his son. How he explained them to himself one cannot guess. But the image remained upon its pedestal, intact and glorious. Until the end he worshiped at the altar of his Unknown Father.

Churchill himself said, "I should have got to know my father, which would have been a joy to me."

Carter, *Winston Churchill: An Intimate Portrait*, 14.

Moments of Comfort

Quotations Worth Remembering: The Mourning
Take this sorrow to thy heart, and make it a part of Thee, and it shall nourish thee till thou art strong again.

Henry Wadsworth Longfellow, *Hyperion*

I believe that a family lives but a half life until it has sent its forerun-
ners into the heavenly world, until those who linger here can cross
the river, and fold transfigured a glorious form in the embrace of an
endless life.

John Bridgman

Good Hamlet, cast thy nighted colour off,
And let thine eye look like a friend on Denmark.
Do not for ever with thy vailed lids
Seek for thy noble father in the dust:
Thou know'st 'tis common; all that lives must die,
Passing through nature to eternity.
William Shakespeare, *Hamlet, 1.2.68–74*

The Bible does not deny the reality of suffering and evil. Neither of
them are excluded from its pages in either the stories of the heroes and
heroines or in the stories of those who seem to be only tragic victims.
But in the face of all the mishaps and misfortunes that have come
along to befall the human race, the Bible continues to affirm that he
will get us home.

Bob Benson, *See You at the House*

There is a loneliness one experiences in the face of death, the loneliness
of having to die one's own death just as one has to live one's own life,
the loneliness of having to live and die alone.

John Donne, *The Reasons of the Heart*

Grieving is as natural as crying when you are hurt, sleeping when you
are tired, eating when you are hungry, or sneezing when your nose
itches. It's nature's way of healing a broken heart.

Don't let anyone take your grief away from you. You deserve it,
and you must have it. If you had broken a leg, no one would criticize
you for using crutches until it was healed. If you had major surgery, no
one would pressure you to run in a marathon the next week. Grief is a

major wound. It does not heal overnight. You must have the time and the crutches until you heal.

Doug Manning, *Don't Take My Grief Away*

"Who says that time heals?" There is a silent, knifelike terror that keeps recurring. You are not only grieving for the person who died, but for yourself, your sense of loss. You keep telling yourself that you must face life without your loved one.

Psychologists call this approach "withdrawing the emotional capital of the past." You do not disregard the person who died. Memories should never be forgotten. But you realize that yesterday with its joys and sorrows has ended. All that it holds of your life is in the treasure-house of the past. There are beautiful reminiscences—sweet and tender. They were yours, but now they are over.

Earl A. Grollman, *Talking About Death*

If death is what it seems to be, and if life beyond is what it seems to be, your loved one has begun a new adventure. How could that person feel resentment toward you? How could he feel cheated? How could he want you punished? He is in a new adventure far greater than yours. You did not cheat the person—nor cause him to miss life. There is no guilt on that side of death—why should there be guilt on this side?

Doug Manning, *Don't Take My Grief Away*

Time, they say, heals. Time also ambushes.
Leighton Ford

What the bereaved person needs desperately is consolation. He also needs courage and hope. He needs love. Let me say, right here at the beginning, that while there are many sources of these things, one towers above all the rest like a great mountain above the lesser foothills. That source is religious faith, belief in the infinite goodness of God who has made none of His processes terrible—not even death—and in the promises of immortality that He has given us.

So when death does come and touch the elbow of someone and deliver the invitation, I prefer to think of him as a friend, gentle and sympathetic, or perhaps as a guide, wise and understanding, who will led me to the Sender of the invitation.

Norman Vincent Peale, *The Healing of Sorrow*

Death can either lead you to the edge of the abyss and threaten your existence with a meaninglessness and futility; or you will start to build the bridge that spans the chasm with things of life that still count—memory, family, friendship, love. When you have sorted out your own feelings, you will be better able to understand your troubled children who come to you laden with questions and beset with fears.

Earl A. Grollman, *Talking About Death*

Scriptures That Comfort
>   It is normal to hurt.

>   My heart is severely pained within me,
>   And the terrors of death have fallen upon me.
>   Fearfulness and trembling have come upon me,
>   And horror has overwhelmed me.
>   And I said, "Oh, that I had wings like a dove!
>   For then I would fly away and be at rest.
>   Indeed, I would wander far off
>   And remain in the wilderness. Selah
>   I would hasten my escape
>   From the windy storm and tempest.
>   *Ps. 55:4–8*

How could Jesus understand my pain?

When Jesus saw her weeping, and the Jews who came with her weeping, He groaned in the spirit and was troubled. And He said, "Where have you laid him?" They said to Him, "Lord, come and see." Jesus wept. Then the Jews said, "See how He loved him!"
John 11:33–36

I don't think I have strength to make it through this.

Have you not known?
Have you not heard?
The everlasting God, the LORD
The Creator of the ends of the earth,
Neither faints nor is weary.
There is no searching of His understanding.
He gives power to the weak,
And to those who have no might
   He increases strength.
Even the youths shall faint and be weary,
And the young men shall utterly fall,
But those who wait on the LORD
Shall renew their strength;
They shall mount up with wings like eagles,
They shall run and not be weary,
They shall walk and not faint.
   Isa. 40:28–31

God understands our emotions.

God will wipe away every tear from their eyes; there shall be no more death, nor sorrow, nor crying; and there shall be no more pain, for the former things have passed away. Then He who sat on the throne said, "Behold, I make all things new."
Rev. 21:4–5

A promise for you, today.

The righteous cry out, and the LORD hears,
And delivers them out of all their troubles.
The LORD is near to those who have a broken heart.
    Ps. 34:17–18

The Lord is present.

And it will be said in that day:
"Behold, this is our God;
We have waited for Him,
    and He will save us.
This is the LORD;
We have waited for Him;
We will be glad and rejoice
    in His salvation."
    Isa. 25:9

But what about tomorrow?

Fear not, for I am with you;
Be not dismayed, for I am your God.
I will strengthen you,
Yes, I will help you,
I will uphold you with My righteous right hand.
    Isa. 41:10

The security of those who have fallen asleep.

But I do not want you to be ignorant, brethren, concerning those who have fallen asleep, lest you sorrow as others who have no hope. For if we believe that Jesus died and rose again, even so God will bring with Him those who sleep in Jesus. For this we say to you by the word of the Lord, that we who are alive and remain until the coming of the Lord will by no means precede those who are asleep. For the Lord Himself will descend from heaven with a shout, with the voice of an archangel, and with the trumpet of God. And the dead in Christ will rise first. Then we who are alive and remain shall be caught up together with them in the clouds to meet the Lord in the air. And thus we shall always be with the Lord. Therefore comfort one another with these words.

    1 Thess. 4:13–18

Hymns That Comfort

Faith of Our Fathers

Faith of our fathers, living still
In spite of dungeon, fire, and sword!
Oh, how our hearts beat high with joy
Whene'er we hear that glorious word!

Our fathers, chained in prisons dark,
Were still in heart and conscience free.
How sweet would be their children's fate
If they, like them, could die for thee!

Faith of our fathers! we will love
Both friend and foe in all our strife;
And preach thee, too, as love knows how,
By kindly words and virtuous life.

Faith of our fathers! holy faith!
We will be true to thee till death!
Frederick W. Faber, Worship in Song, *413.*

My Faith Looks up to Thee

My faith looks up to Thee,
Thou Lamb of Calvary, Savior divine!

Now hear me while I pray; Take all my guilt away.
Oh, let me from this day
Be wholly Thine!

May Thy rich grace impart,
Strength to my fainting heart, My zeal inspire.
As Thou hast died for me, Oh, may my love to Thee
Pure, warm, and changeless be,
A living fire!

While life's dark maze I tread,
And griefs around me spread, Be Thou my Guide.
Bid darkness turn to day
Wipe sorrow's tears away;
Nor let me ever stray From Thee aside!

When ends life's transient dream,
And death's cold, sullen stream, Shall o'er me roll,
Blest Savior, then, in love,
Fear and distrust remove.
Oh, bear me safe above, A ransomed soul.
Ray Palmer, *Worship in Song,* 54.

For All the Saints

For all the saints who from their labors rest.
Who Thee by faith before the world confessed,
Thy name, O Jesus, be forever blest.
Alleluia! Alleluia.

Thou wast their rock, their fortress, and their might;
Thou, Lord, their captain in the well-fought fight;
Thou, in the darkness drear, their one true light.
Alleluia! Alleluia.

O blest communion, fellowship divine!
We feebly struggle; they in glory shine.
Yet all are one in Thee, for all are Thine.
Alleluia! Alleluia.

And when the strife is fierce, the warfare long,
Steals on the ear the distant triumph song,
And hearts are brave again and arms are strong,
Alleluia! Alleluia.

The golden evening brightens in the west;
Soon, soon to faithful warriors cometh rest;
And sweet the calm of Paradise, the blest.
Alleluia! Alleluia.

But Lo! there breaks a yet more glorious day;
The saints trimphant rise in bright array;
The King of Glory passed on His way.
Alleluia! Alleluia.

From earth's wide bounds, from ocean's farthest coast,
Thru' gates of pearl stream in the countless host,
Singing to Father, Son, and Holy Ghost.
Alleluia! Alleluia.
William W. How, Crusader Hymns.

Prayers That Comfort

Grant to all who mourn a sure confidence in thy fatherly care, that, casting all their grief on thee, they may know the consolation of thy love. *Amen.*

   Book of Common Prayer

Help us, we pray, in the midst of things we cannot understand, to believe and trust in the communion of the saints, the forgiveness of sins, and the resurrection to life everlasting. *Amen.*

Book of Common Prayer

O God of grace and glory, we remember before you this day our father. We thank you for giving him to us, his family and friends, to know and to love as a companion on our earthly pilgrimage. In your boundless compassion, console us who mourn. Give us faith to see in death the gate of eternal life, so that in quiet confidence we may continue our course on earth, until, by your call, we are reunited with those who have gone before; through Jesus Christ our Lord. *Amen.*

Book of Common Prayer

Grant, O Lord, to all who are bereaved the spirit of faith and courage, that they may have strength to meet the days to come with steadfastness and patience; not sorrowing as those without hope, but in thankful remembrance of your great goodness, and in the joyful expectation of eternal faith with those they love. And this we ask in the name of Jesus Christ our savior. *Amen.*

Book of Common Prayer

Almighty God, Father of mercies and giver of comfort: Deal graciously, we pray, with all who mourn that, casting all their care on you, they may know the consolation of your love; through Jesus Christ our Lord. *Amen.*

Book of Common Prayer

A prayer for daily strength.

O God,
Help me to live one day at a time,

not to be thinking of what might have been
    and not to be worrying about what may be.
Help me to accept the fact
    that I cannot undo the past,
    and I cannot foresee the future.
But even as I think of this,
    and even as I face today,
Help me always to remember
    that I will never be tried beyond what I can bear;
    that a father's hand will never cause
    his child a needless tear;
    that I cannot ever drift
    beyond your love and care.
So help me to live today
    in courage, in cheerfulness and in peace.
This I ask for Jesus' sake. *Amen.*
Barclay, *Prayers for Help and Healing.*

A prayer for when my thoughts are confused.

Thou great Lord of all mystery, if in the presence of death our thoughts are startled and our words flutter in all directions like frightened birds, bring us stillness that we may cover the sorrow of our hearts with folded hands.

Give us grace to wait on thee, silently and with patience. Thou art nearer to us than we know, nearer than we can think. If we cannot find thee it is because we search in far places.

Thou who dost walk in the valley of every shadow, be thou our good Shepherd and sustain us while we walk with thee, lest in weakness we falter.

Though the pain deepens, keep us in thy way and guide us past every danger, through Jesus Christ our Lord. *Amen.*
Miller, *Prayers for Daily Use,* 128.

A prayer after hearing Handel's Messiah.

Our Father, in the midst of our sorrow and defeat we would hear again that triumphant shout, "The kingdoms of this world have become the kingdoms of our Lord and of his Christ, and he shall reign for ever and ever." Help us to find comfort in the certainty of this victory. Give us the faith to live each moment of each day in the assurance of our Christian hope; for we pray in Jesus' name. *Amen*

Baird and Baird, *Funeral Meditations,* 112.

4

THE REMEMBERING

Eternity is increasingly a world that i am attracted to.

Bob Buford

When It Hurt Him the Most

I THINK HIS illness hurt him the most when he was too weak to carry my suitcase at the airport. We argued about it, and I saw a flash of the old Dad. "No, it's too heavy," I announced.

"I can carry it!" he retorted.

So although I knew my suitcase was too heavy, I let him carry it to the car, his pride intact.

That's when this thing called illness seemed so outrageous: when proud old men can't do those things they once never gave a thought to. My dad had the strength of an ox, but now. . . .

And what seemed even more outrageous was that it seemed only yesterday he had spoken those same words, "It's too heavy," to me, and I had, although just a boy, as resolutely answered, "I can carry it!"

As a father gave in then, I now gave in. Of course, as we walked from baggage to the car, I got a few "looks" from strangers: "Why is that big guy letting that old man carry that heavy suitcase?"

I'm not sure they would have understood my answer.

Exchanged Roles

I'll never forget the day we exchanged roles during his illness; he, the child; I, the parent.

That miserable December morning, we soft-shoed those few feet from his hospital bed to the chair by the window. The whole time I agonized that he might slip from my embrace and break his hip. Or worse.

Fatigued after the first few steps, he laid his head against my neck. I felt his exhaustion. I felt his anguish. I felt his humiliation.

Only a few years ago, he had helped me walk. How tightly I had gripped his hand then. Now it was my turn to lead, his turn to trust.

That once strong man, who once had worked endless days and nights, now sat staring out his window into the December gray, exhausted by a few steps.

Why bother? The doctors had said that he *had* to get up. He *had* to walk. He *had* to get well. Our little ballet was part of the process. But he knew and I knew the truth. He wouldn't get well.

Suffering

It was so hard for me to see him suffering. To see him stripped of his strength. To see the pleading in his eyes. This once strong man, now a feeble, frail shell of what he had been: robust, healthy, strong.

Every time I saw him and measured the loss since the last time, I recognized that would someday be me. I recall the cemetery tombstone that captured my curiosity:

As you are
So once was I.
As I now am
So soon you shall be.
Prepare for death
And follow me.

No Fear

My father had no fear of death. None. He'd seen the death angel too many times in his years of working with high voltage electricity.

Now as he awaited the tardy death angel, my father believed that what lay ahead, although unknown, was better than what was.

My father possessed a simple faith that asked few questions and demanded few answers, but provided far more confidence for him than my faith has provided me.

What did my dad know that I don't? Is there any way to know other than through suffering?

Conversations

Even if my mom remarried (and she won't) there will never be another Dad. He was the original that they broke the mold on. You would have loved him; most people did. Oh, he would have asked you questions and said, "Can't you stay a spell?" He always preferred words like *spell,* and that drove his educated son crazy at times.

And sooner or later, he would have offered you some of his opinions on subjects of common interest. Then he would have listened to yours. He would have considered you a nice person and hoped, out loud, that you would come back when you could stay longer.

Strangers, to my daddy, were only the people he hadn't talked to—yet. And he would have asked you, once he found out where you were from, if you knew So-and-So. Or what are they saying over there about _____? Or what kind of weather do you have in those parts?

And eventually, for certain, he would have mentioned the Big '37 Hood (it was THE big one, you know). And if you didn't know, after a respectful but thorough explanation, you would have known that that flood had been a big event in his life.

And my mother had learned that when he was late, he probably had gotten to talking to someone and would be home "directly," which was never a direction but a measure of time.

My dad was such a talker that I doubt he got much sleep the first week he was in heaven. He found it a good time to catch up with his friends.

And I have a feeling that a lot of folks miss having my dad around to listen to them. Because not many people these days will listen to your stories all the way to the end. They listen awhile, then interrupt. Not my dad. In those last years, he couldn't chop firewood or hoe his garden or shovel snow, but he could still listen.

And a lot of folks, including me, had lighter hearts after twenty minutes of talking with my dad.

There were those special conversations that, for whatever reason, were just between the two of us. Special. Privileged. Almost as if there were a "No Trespassing" sign posted. He never thought of telling my mother. And when she would ask what we had talked about, as she would, he'd say, "Oh, nothing much. . . "

Nothing much wasn't meant to discount the conversation but to lighten Mom's anxiety.

But I suspect that some nights in that big old bed they had shared for five decades, he would tell her a little of it. Enough to dampen her curiosity, but not enough to arouse her apprehension.

Some things he did share with her, simply because his soul wasn't big enough to carry them alone. When my wife left me and my heart was broken, his heart was broken too.

But some important things he took to his grave, unspoken.

Lately, I find myself wishing that I had time to talk with him again about some things. Like turning forty. I'm not sure he would have understood all my concern, because when he was forty he had not only three children but a grandchild. Dad didn't have time to have a "midlife crisis." But I think just talking it over with him would have done me good.

In moments like this, I am reminded that the world is different because I have no father to talk to. But there are some ways to communicate. I have a friend with a Harvard Ph.D., who, when he runs up against something his Harvard education can't solve, goes out to his father's grave and talks.

A couple of other friends write letters to their fathers. They never mail them. And another says that he talks to his dad in his mind. I thought that was crazy until my dad died. Now it makes a lot of sense.

And some days, I find myself saying things and stopping midsentence, things that sound just like my father.

That's one reason I like people who say, "You know, my father used to say. . . ." Even though you can't talk to him, you can remember those unique little phrases that were his.

My dad, even in deathbed hallucinations, would threaten "to take a clapboard" to someone. I never saw a clapboard that I can remember, but the way my dad talked about its secondary use, I never wanted to.

Some days, I have a hard time remembering what his voice sounded like. Yet on other days, I hear a voice and feel my heartbeat stop because it sounds so much like him.

Autumn Leaves

It is my first autumn without my dad.

I have watched the leaves in East Tennessee and West Virginia and North Carolina do their fall routines. Colors that even I as a writer cannot fully describe. I have watched them in my backyard, too.

Autumn leaves are becoming quite an industry. Places in the East now enjoy a second season for tourists who come to gawk at the leaves.

The leaves are dead. But the way we deal with their dying is that we know, come springtime, the leaves will return. And we know that next fall Mother Nature will put on another show in the timeless pageant of autumn beauty.

It was about this time of year that my dad got the maddest with me that I can remember. Seventh grade. Suda East Butler School. I had a science project. On leaves.

For some reason that I cannot remember, I had delayed the gathering until the last minute. I had to have forty varieties of leaves, pronto.

So one fall afternoon, my dad went on a little hike through the 150 acres of woods behind our house carefully collecting leaves, sticking them into pinprick holes in a sheet of cardboard. Under each he wrote the name.

Great! Thanks, Dad.

By about 9:00 P.M. I had a mess on my hands. To rearrange them, I had taken them out of their cardboard niches. They were strewn all across my bedroom. I couldn't tell a maple from an oak.

But I discovered something that night. My dad couldn't either, without seeing the tree. Maybe the dilemma would not have become a full-blown crisis if my mother had not started second-guessing some of my dad's reidentifications. "Oh, that's not a maple leaf!"

My dad kept asking, "Why did you take them out of the cardboard?" How could I tell him that the presentation had to look sharp? That neatness and display counted toward my grade as much as the number of leaves?

I never asked my dad's help after that. Even if it meant a C.

But I do appreciate leaves, more so after they are dead. And I know that my dad liked autumn for its colors and smells.

I have decided that that's what eternity is: springtime after earth's autumn.

On Remembering

Humankind is uniquely gifted with a keen memory. The words "In remembrance" appear on sympathy cards, on service folders.

In this section, we look at how a group of sons/daughters remember their father. Often it requires a choice on the son's or daughter's part. To balance the good against the painful. Some choose to deny the bad and deliberately remember only the good. That choice may compound the grieving process and delay healing.

However, when the relationships were strong and supportive and warm, the son or daughter may choose to focus on a particular memory.

George Bush *was serving his country as US Ambassador to the United Nations as his father died of cancer. Mr. Bush wrote these words for Father's Day 1972. Four months later his father died.*

When I think of my Dad I think of strength and deep conviction. I think of love of country and public service. I think of common decency. Ever since we Bush sons have been old enough to remember, people have said, "You must be Pres Bush's boy." Perhaps they knew him as a business leader or as a distinguished U.S. Senator; or in athletics in which he excelled; or in any of a number of human causes he so unselfishly served. Or perhaps they know him now, somewhat retired, but still active, still concerned, still caring deeply. They might have been men of great power or simple, humble people, but in whatever way they knew him then, or know him now, there is always respect, always affection for my Dad. In a time when the fundamental values that have guided my Dad's life are under attack—values of family, religion, respect of law, compassion for one's fellow human being—I get continuing strength from my father's love, from my father's life, yes, from being "Pres Bush's boy."

"Saturday Journal," *New Haven Register,* 17 June 1972, 16.

A father's courage can stimulate great courage in his offspring. On February 28, 1944, in Nazi-occupied Haarlem, the Netherlands, Casper ten Boom, and his daughters Corrie and Betsy were arrested, charged with hiding Jews. Betsy and her father died in prison, and Corrie was sent to Ravensbruck, known as "the concentration camp of no return." Through a bureaucratic mix-up, she was released days before she was scheduled to be executed.

Imagine the stress on this woman in the early days of her imprisonment, not knowing the status of her elderly father. Two months after his death, she learned that he had died in a hospital corridor without medical assistance. Corrie ten Boom was fifty-two and faced rebuilding her life without her family.

In Scheveningen we were brought to the Bureau of the Gestapo. My sister said to the officers, "My father is so ill and weak he will not be able to take that high step into the auto."

As father was carried into the Bureau a German said, "You might as well let that man die at home."

"What!" yelled the captain. "That man is the worst of them all. He talks about nothing but Jesus and the Queen."

It was quite a distance from the Bureau to the prison, and we were shoved into a patrol car. It reminded me of the tumbrils in the stories of the French Revolution. It was a horrible vehicle, without springs, and jolted continually. Father lay in my arms. Even one of the officers helped to support him to ease the worst jobs.

And then the gate of the great prison closed behind us.

"Alle nasen gegen mauer!" (Every nose to the wall!) And there we stood facing the wall. Father was allowed to sit on a chair. I pressed a kiss to his forehead, that noble forehead.

"The Lord be with you," I whispered.

"And with you," was his reply.

I turned and looked back once more. It was my last glimpse of father on earth. He was to survive his arrest by only ten days. In the cell he was reported to have been very courageous, saying to his cellmates: "If I am released tomorrow I shall go on the day after tomorrow giving aid to the Jews and shelter and help to all who need it."

Long afterwards I learned that during his last days his mind was confused. He was brought to a hospital where he died in the corridor. They buried him in a pauper's grave. When he died his children and youngest grandson were in the same prison. What little effort it would have required to bring us to him. But we were not allowed to even know that he had died.

People had often warned Father, "If you persist in harboring as many Jews you will eventually end up in prison, and in your delicate condition you could never survive that."

And Father would answer, "If that should come to pass I shall consider it an honor to give my life for God's ancient people."

That honor had now been bestowed upon him. Father had died in prison, a martyr's death.

A Prisoner and Yet, 21–22.

Last conversations are important memories for sons and daughters. Things we said as well as things we wish we had said or had not said long influence the grieving process. Beverly Sills particularly remembers her last conversation with her father. She had dropped by to visit him in the hospital on her way to a concert:

I remember I wore a black strapless dress when I went to visit Papa in the hospital. He looked at me and said, "You look wonderful. Don't let yourself get fat."

I laughed and said, "Why do you think I'll let myself get fat?"

"Because you like ice cream too much," he said. . . .

The truth of the matter is that I always have liked ice cream a lot. And crazy as it sounds, I never take a bite of ice cream without thinking of him. Never.

Beverly: An Autobiography, 45.

Sometimes, consequences of a father's death come years later. David Gordon, father of the highly acclaimed novelist, Mary Gordon, died in 1956 when Mary was seven. Five years later she made a discovery about her father's past that forever haunted her.

He [her father] published a girlie magazine called *Hot Dog.* I remember being twelve, and my father had died when I was seven, and I came upon this magazine while looking through his pictures. By today's standards it's exceedingly mild, and I took a look at this thing and I saw that my father had been the editor, and I was appalled and I ripped it to shreds and threw it away.

Zinsser, ed., *Spiritual Quests,* 36.

Some fathers, even in dying, have the ability to reach deep within themselves to complete some task or assignment. That struggle becomes the valued memory of their children. Robert Benson, a public relations consultant, remembers such an event in his father's life. Bob Benson, book publisher and author, died on March 22, 1986, at age fifty-five.

Robert was thirty-three at the time of his father's death.

There is one Bob Benson story here that you won't find anywhere else. He never had a chance to tell it. That's because it is one he and I whispered back and forth to each other in the spring on one of the last times that I saw him. He might not have ever gotten around to telling it anyway, since he was the hero in it.

Last year, just after Christmas, well before any of us (except perhaps he himself) knew just how ill he was becoming, the family trooped their way up to the Smokies for a belated Christmas vacation together. My dad was always a big vacation planner, usually figuring out a plan that involved several cars and numerous stops for meals and neat little places to stay. Some of our best memories of "home" didn't take place at home at all; they happened on some beach or in some city far away or beside an interstate highway when we all got so tickled at each other we could hardly stand it. . . .

. . . So, dad and Leigh [my sister] and I set out to climb the Chimneys together. Actually, more climbers than that started out with us. . . . Troopers though they were, there was a little more ice and snow still up there than they needed, and they headed back.

But Leigh and Dad and I pressed on. And to be honest it was a struggle for Dad. People with asthma don't always make good climbers, and Dad wasn't very strong to boot. So it took us a while in the snow and ice. But we made it.

We didn't stay up there very long, since we had taken most of the afternoon light coming up and we were afraid to let it get too dark before we started back down. But there was time for an apple or two and a candy bar that we had saved for the occasion; and so we sat for a few minutes together. Nobody said much, we all just kept grinning at each other. And we snapped what was left of a roll of film that I had, just in case we needed proof later on that we hadn't bailed out along the way.

The next day, we all kind of packed up in a hurry and headed our various ways. A few days later, the next time I saw my dad, he had spoken for what was to be the last time, and he was about to check into the hospital for what was to be the last time.

I took the pictures we had shot on the mountain to show Dad one night not long after the doctors had gathered us all together to tell us that he wouldn't be coming home to us again. The doctors saw the pictures, too, and couldn't believe that he had even tried the climb, much less finished it. I wasn't surprised much. He spent most of his life climbing up one mountain or another—illness, discouragement, rejection slips, business problems, and the stuff that goes with being a parent to five kids.

I could have told the doctors that my dad was funny like that; he just thought that mountains were for climbing. He also thought songs were for singing and hands were for holding and people were for loving and stories were for telling and life was for living. He may not have been here for long, but he didn't miss much.

I really brought him the pictures because I wanted to be sure that he saw the ones of his granddaughter (and my daughter) on her first climb. In a decidedly uncharacteristic move, he kept looking at the ones of himself standing on the top of Chimney Tops. And I watched him while he watched those pictures as though he could still feel the wind on his face and the sweat in his shirt and the mud on his hands and the pain in his chest from the climb.

After a while, he laid his head back on the pillow and held my hand and whispered, "I'm so glad that I climbed that mountain. I'm so glad I made it to the top. It doesn't matter what it cost me. I did make it to the top, didn't I?"

"Yeah, Dad, you made it to the top. Again. Get some rest, have another apple or two."
See You at the House, introduction.

Despite the urging of insurance companies and financial planners, a father's financial reverses can limit a son's or daughter's educational opportunities and future. Dr. Allen White, physician, druggist, and merchant, died on October 4, 1882. His son, William Allen White, *future winner of two Pulitzer Prizes for writing, was fourteen and quickly realized that his educational opportunities would be limited, but he did not realize what his father* had *given him:*

I understood. . . only when I saw him in the retrospect of my own manhood and middle age. A boy of fourteen could not comprehend such a man as he was. But when my memory put him together again, I could mourn him deeply. I have never ceased to sorrow that he did not stay with me for another twenty years, to help me and to guide me from the follies which he may have seen ahead of me.

White's final words on his father could be echoed in the thoughts of many readers.

I know now what I did not know then—that I was the apple of his eye. He loved me and hoped for me and maybe . . . he prayed for me. And when I was old I did not depart from the way!
An Autobiography of William Allen White, 85.
Some children are destined for great achievement. Yet there may be little at the time of their father's death to indicate their future success. No wonder some grieve with a sense of wishing their fathers could have lived long enough to have witnessed their achievements.
Golda Meir, *prime minister of Israel, regretted that her father, Moshe Mobovitz, died in the 1940s, long before his daughter entered politics.*

Father died at the age of seventy-nine, and until the last six months of his life when he fell ill, he was strong, upright, handsome. During a demonstration in Migdel Father marched a long distance in protest against the British and was always active in the struggle for Jewish labor. Throughout the years he lived in this country he conscientiously performed all the good deeds demanded of Jews in the homeland.

Father died before the establishment of the state of Israel. I have always viewed my membership in the government as a job that had to be done, but I have often thought of what it would have meant to Father if he had lived to see the creation of a Jewish state, with a Jewish government, and with his daughter a member of that government.

To what extent did Father and Mother make me what I am?. . . From my father I got, let us say, my obstinacy. Insofar as I have shown the quality of firmness, it came mainly from him.

A Land of Our Own: An Oral Biography, 36.

Some fathers have sacrificed so much to give their sons and daughters "opportunity." Many left a cherished home country for the new world called America in order to maximize that chance. Nicola Iacocca came to the United States in 1912 as a twelve-year-old wanting a future. He had no inkling that his son, Lido, would grow up to be one of the most powerful businessmen in the twentieth century.

Nicola died in 1973 at age eighty-three.

Lee Iacocca was forty-eight years old when his father died.

My father and I were very close. I loved pleasing him, and he was always terrifically proud of my accomplishments. If I won a spelling contest at school, he was on top of the world. Later in life whenever I got a promotion, I'd call my father right away and he'd rush out to tell all his friends. At Ford, each time I brought out a new car, he wanted to be the first to drive it. In 1970, when I was named president of the Ford Motor Company, I don't know which of us was more excited.

. . . when I look back on my father, I only remember a man of great vigor and boundless energy. Once I was in Palm Springs for a Ford dealer meeting, and I invited my father to come out for a brief vacation. When the meeting was over, a couple of us went out to play golf. Although my father had never been on a golf course in his life, we asked him to come along.

As soon as he hit the ball, he began to chase after it—seventy years old and running all the way. I had to keep reminding him: "Pop, slow down. Golf is a game of *walking!*"

But that was my father for you. He always preached: "Why walk when you can run?"

Iacocca, 4, 12.

Death is not always convenient. It may interrupt happy moments in a family. Bob Dole, *US senator from Kansas, married Elizabeth Hanford on December 6, 1975, in Washington, D.C. His parents had flown from rural town Russell, Kansas, for the occasion and were staying in Senator Dole's Watergate apartment while the couple honeymooned in the Virgin Islands. They must have marveled at their son's success. On December 8, Doran Dole, who had only missed one day of work in forty years, died of a massive heart attack.*

Senator Dole has chosen to remember his father by hanging a large portrait of Doran above his desk in his Senate office. One biographer noted, "There Doran would always be watching over Bob, making sure he worked as hard as possible."

Hilton, *Bob Dole: American Political Phoenix,* 119–120.

Fathers sometimes complicate the lives of their sons. One, for instance, was denounced as a Communist and was convicted of manslaughter when a woman patient died after he performed a therapeutic abortion on her. He served in Sing Sing Prison from 1919 until he was pardoned in 1924.

Such was the legacy for Armand Hammer, industrialist, international financier, whose father, Dr. Julian Hammer, a physician, died on October 17, 1948, at age seventy- four. Young Hammer had worked tirelessly to see that his father's license to practice medicine was restored in 1943.

Armand was fifty years old when his father died. What did Julian Hammer leave his son? Two things:

One of my father's most precious legacies to me was spiritual. I learned from him the value of courage and the strength of will. He taught me that despondency and despair can be overcome by determination. During those middle years of my life, . . . I often felt I had bitten off more than I could chew; I was frequently subject to bouts of despondency. My usual optimism would give way to dark pessimism, hope would be replaced by despair, daring by uncertainty, and courage by defeatism and fear.

But in those times,

I would try to remember the maxims by which my father had sustained his own courage through his troubles.

The second gift was an interest in the search for a cure for cancer, a cause in which Dr. Hammer invests several million dollars each year.

My passion on this subject came about as a kind of living memorial to the medical work of my father. I have never forgotten the misery and sense of hopelessness my father felt as he battled the polio epidemic in the early decades of this century. He felt a cure for that dreadful scourge would never be discovered—and yet it was, by Dr. Jonas Salk in 1955. Several generations have now grown to adulthood free from the menace of that mutilating and killing sickness.

My father considered polio to be as incurable then as many people suppose cancer to be today—as if it were a rogue development of nature that is beyond the powers of human beings to control or defeat. I have never shared that pessimism.
Hammer, 283–486.

Sometimes, fathers have a capacity to influence their sons after death. The Scriptures talk of those who "being dead still speeds..." (Heb. 11:4).
Carl Lewis *is considered by many to be the fastest male runner in the world. He had long been influenced by his father, William Lewis, who died in May 1987, at age sixty. Carl was twenty-six.*

Carl Lewis won four gold medals in the 1984 Los Angeles Olympics: the 100-yard, 200-yard, 4 x 100-yard relays, and the long jump. His father, founder of the Willingboro track club, beamed when he talked about his son's future and as he looked toward Seoul. Could Carl duplicate his feat in 1988?

He won the long jump but didn't set a record. He was upset in the 200-yard by his teammate and close friend, Joe DeLoach. His chance of winning a gold in relay was eliminated when the U.S. team was disqualified. Then his attention focused on the 100-yard run on Saturday evening; the world would be watching because he was pitted against Canadian best, Ben Johnson. Could he beat Johnson?

The race had a particular meaning because Lewis no longer had the 100-yard gold medal from 1984. At his father's funeral, he had slipped the medal between his father's fingers and said, "You keep it. I'll get another one." His father had been buried with the gold medal.

Moreover, on September 27, 1988, Carl Lewis spoke at a Lay Witnesses for Christ rally in a Seoul church and shared his mother's dream from the night before the 100-yard final.

"My father came to her in her dream. He told her to make sure that I knew he was proud of me, and that whatever performance I made, don't worry about it. He said that everything would be all right. He said it again; everything would be all right."

The pressure was enormous. But Lewis knew that he could beat Ben Johnson; he had beat him in the 100-yard in Zurich a few weeks earlier. But this was for the gold medal; a silver medal wouldn't do.

As the world knows, Ben Johnson decisively beat Carl Lewis. The cameras focused on a dejected Lewis who walked back to the dressing room.

However, the world was stunned when Johnson was stripped of his medal for using steroids. In private ceremonies, Carl Lewis was awarded the gold after all.

William Lewis had continued to influence his son. Fifteen months before Carl had said, "This is going to be my best year, and my father is going to be there watching. . . . He's not gone, he's just watching from another place."

Jet, 25 May 1987; 1 June 1987; *Sports Illustrated*, 10 October 1988.

Pinchus Joseph Herman Greenberg ran a bakeshop in a poor neighborhood in Brooklyn, New York, during the Depression. Often, he slipped a few buns or cakes into the bags of customers who could only afford bread. If the customer mentioned it the next time in the bakery, Mr. Greenberg would say, "A little mistake. Forget it, please." . . . Greenberg died in November 1963, and his son, Michael Greenberg, wanted to find a way to pay tribute to his father's generosity.

Mike, a media analyst for Grey Advertising in New York City, remembered that in the Depression days when the family was struggling, if he lost his gloves, "Money was scarce; I was ashamed to ask for a new pair."

After his father's death, Mike started buying three pairs of warm gloves every payday, twice a month, winter and summer. For twenty-five years, between Thanksgiving and Hanukkah-Christmas, Mike has given dozens of pairs of gloves in the city's Bowery District to the homeless who live on the street.

Although no one in the Bowery knows Mike's name, he is nicknamed "Gloves."

Guideposts, December 1985, 15–16; *Time*, 2 January 1989, 16–21, 23.

Moments of Comfort

Quotations Worth Remembering: The Remembering

I believe in eternal life. I believe we live on after this life is over—in a new and better life beyond death. I believe we also live on in the lives of those we have touched.

If I understand the Bible, persons give glory to God. He made us and is proud of what He made. Whatever we have become gives glory to Him. I think we pay the ultimate homage to God when we celebrate the life of one of His creations.

Doug Manning, *Don't Take My Grief Away*

And so I like the Bible
  because it ends well.
It begins with the heroes
  in a sinless, deathless land—
But they tripped, fell, and got lost on
  a downward journey that led through
  sin, misery, failure,
  sorrow, war and shame.
And finally you begin to think
  they are never going to
  make it back.
But when it ends,
  they are at home again—
  in a sinless, deathless land.
It took God's son to do it—
  but it ends well.

Bob Benson, *He Speaks Softly*

I'm just a bit player too
  not a star in any way—
But God gave me a line or so
  in the pageant of life,

and when the curtain falls
and the drama ends—
and the stage is vacant at last
I don't ask for a critic's raves
or fame in any amount.
I only hope he can say,
"He said his lines,
Not too soon, not too late,
not too loud, not too soft.
He said his lines
and he said them well."
Robert Benson, *See You at the House*

Scripture That Comforts

To everything there is a season,
A time for every purpose under heaven:
A time to be born,
And a time to die;
A time to plant,
And a time to pluck what is planted;
A time to kill,
And a time to heal;
A time to break down,
And a time to build up;
A time to weep,
And a time to laugh;
A time to mourn,
And a time to dance;
A time to cast away stones,
And a time to gather stones;
A time to embrace,
And a time to refrain from embracing;
A time to gain,

And a time to lose;
A time to keep,
And a time to throw away;
A time to tear,
And a time to sew;
A time to keep silence,
And a time to speak;
A time to love,
And a time to hate;
A time of war,
And a time of peace.
Ecc. 3:1–8

Prayers That Comfort
Remembering our loss.

O God of Life, in whom there is no death and in whose presence we are called to live as immortal spirits, our thoughts turn to loved ones whom we greatly miss. Their absence has taken from us a treasure the world cannot restore. Yesterday they were with us; now they are with Thee.

The rocks endure though centuries pass away; the ancient hills look down upon a thousand generations; the stars shone on man in his infancy and will shine beyond his little day.

O Thou who art able to guide the suns in their courses, mold the granite of the mountain ranges, and bring life to birth, Thou wilt not let Thy children pass into endless night, their highest hopes unfulfilled.

Still our human needs fill us with loneliness when our beloved go from our sight into the unknown. Thou hast overcome the grave, O Christ; in Thee death is swallowed up in victory. Ten thousand times ten thousand sing the praise of Him who has opened the gates of the City of God.

Praise be unto God who holds our loved ones in His mighty keeping and whose love enfolds them everyone. *Amen.*

Harlow, in *The Funeral Encyclopedia*, 285.

Thanks for a godly father.

O Thou who art the lord of life and yet our father:

We thank Thee for the revelation of Thyself in the lives of those we know best, and especially for the evidence of Thy presence in the life, of this Thy child now recalled to be with Thee. Those who have known him as father thank Thee for his strength and courage in the face of difficulty; for his wisdom and kindly guidance, for the sacrifice that was his daily living. His friends praise Thee for his friendly and generous spirit that made him loved by young and old; for the qualities of goodness that made him share what he had of spiritual and material blessings with all. For all these things and in the more personal relationships of the spirit we lift our voices in praise.

Thou hast in Thy providence called him to be with Thee in that larger life beyond the grave. We have shared his life and now we give him back to Thee in the full assurance that this life fulfilled here will find a new expression and will accept new responsibility as Thou dost give them to him.

Give each of us, our Father, a larger understanding of our relationship to Thee and to all of life. Help us as we contemplate the qualities of righteousness seen in this Thy servant, to catch the challenge of his life and to prepare ourselves by the working out of Thy will for us, that in that day when we shall be called Thou canst say of us, "Well done, thou good and faithful servant, thou hast been faithful over few things, I will make thee ruler of many."

In Christ's name we pray. *Amen.*

Harding, in *The Funeral Encyclopedia*, 283.

A prayer and reminder.

We remember, Lord, the slenderness of the thread which separates life from death, and the suddenness with which it can be broken. Help us also to remember that on both sides of that division we are surrounded by your love.

Persuade our hearts that when our dear ones die neither we nor they are parted from you.

In you may we find peace, and in you be united with them in the body of Christ, who has burst the bonds of death and is alive for evermore, our Savior and theirs for ever and ever. *Amen.*

Williams, in *The New Book of Christian Prayers,* 236.

A prayer for grace.

God be in my head
And in my understanding.
God be in mine eyes
And in my looking.
God be in my mouth
And in my speaking.
God be in my heart
And in my thinking.
God be at mine end
And at my departing.

Sarum Prayer, in *The New Book of Christian Prayers,* 97.

A prayer for courage to follow Dad's footsteps.

A Lord God of our fathers, we bless thy holy Name, thy grace and mercy for all those who have gone before us to rest in thee; all, in all vocations, who have pleased thee. And, we pray thee, give us also grace to walk before thee as they walked, in righteousness and self-denial, that, having laboured as they laboured, we may afterwards rest as they rest. *Amen.*

Rossetti, *in Handbook of Public Prayer,* 188–189.

A prayer to remind me of the need for preparation.

O Thou that hast prepared a place for my soul, prepare my soul for that place; prepare it with holiness; prepare it with desire; and even while it sojourneth upon earth, let it dwell in heaven with thee; beholding the beauty of thy countenance and glory of thy saints, now and forevermore. *Amen.*

Hall, in *Handbook of Public Prayer,* 149.

5

FROM NOW TILL ETERNITY

Each departed one is a magnet that attracts us to the next world.

John Richter

It's Been a Year

THEY SAY THAT once you turn forty the year passes much more swiftly.

I think that once you've buried your father the year passes even more swiftly.

I am sitting here asking myself how one year could have passed so quickly. A year ago today my dad died. I remember as a child how impatient I was with time, how many times I drove my dad up the wall, when in response to his promise, "When I get time" I would ask, for the millionth time, "Is it time, *yet?*"

I thought Sunday afternoons were forever. I thought naps were forever. I thought school was forever. It seemed that it took forever to be my birthday or Christmas.

In my heart, it seems as if only yesterday I talked with him. And now my datebook says it's been a year and a day.

Is this how it is to be the rest of my life?

Joining the Fraternity

There are some who strongly disagree with my contention
   that a father's death is different from a mother's.
   Definitely different.
Some would argue, almost as convincingly, that a parent's

death, whether father or mother, is traumatic.

Some of the problem could be semantic. How can I put into
language the mourning of my heart? How can anyone comprehend if they have not experienced this particular loss?

Only when the loss is real can anyone argue the question.

But one thing is certain: funerals are far more serious for me
now that my father has had one. Now that I have "been
there."

For in becoming a mourner, I joined a unique human group:
the fatherless.

But, I am also aware that he awaits that certain morning,
perhaps evening, when I too shall slip free of all that binds
me to earth and step into eternity. And I will recognize
my dad. And no previous moment in my life will match
that one.

See You at Home

My dad was a hard-working man. Still he never scraped enough money
together to make a down payment on a house until he was forty-two
years old. I made it when I was thirty-two, which proves something of
upward mobility.

We rented a comfortable house at the corner of 25th and Howard
with a great backyard that stimulated my curiosity. From the kitchen window my mother could watch me walk to Brandeis Elementary School.
I felt snug in that neighborhood. Dutch Meissner's grocery story—with
his rows of penny candy and colored iced donuts—was only two blocks
away; the church we attended was just up the street. There was a big
empty lot next door for baseball games and dirtclod fights.

Everything was going pretty well in my five-year-old world until
my dad bought a house in a new development in what was then "country." I was absolutely set against the idea. I liked 25th and Howard.
I still remember the Sunday my parents bought 4809 Beech Drive.

I announced I was going to stay at 25th and Howard. I can still hear my family's laughter.

But eventually the idea sank in that we were going to move. I didn't like it. I sulked and whined and risked a direct confrontation with my father's belt.

Eventually moving day came. Fighting back tears, I said good-bye to all my pals and watched the house emptied. Finally, I ran outside and sat on the big concrete retaining wall. Crying.

I can still remember my dad in his truck turning the corner onto 25th Street and finding me. "What's wrong?" he asked.

"Daddy, where we gonna sleep tonight?"

"At home!" he announced.

"Daddy, *this* is home," I protested.

"No, Harold. This is Mr. Lipp's house. We've only been renting. Now, we have a place all our own."

"But, Daddy, I want to stay *here.*"

My dad ordinarily was not one to prolong pointless conversations. He had a truckful of furniture to move so that eight people would have a place to sleep in a few hours.

He drove away. For some reason, not quite out of my teary eyesight, he stuck his head out the window and yelled back, "I'll see you at home."

A couple of hours later, I slept on the couch, made into a bed, at 4809 Beech Drive. Slowly, I got used to the idea that the days at 25th and Howard were over. But my dad only considered 4809 Beech Drive his address. Home was where his Father was waiting. That's the way I think of heaven now. As home.

I thought about that as I flew to Louisville to conduct my father's funeral.

When I closed my dad's funeral and it was time for that last walk by the casket, I turned from the little podium and faced the casket and said, "Dad, I'll see you *at home.*"

And by the grace of God, I intend to do just that.

SOURCES

The following sources are acknowledged:

Chapter 1

Roosevelt, James, with Bill Libby. *My Parents: A Differing View*. Chicago: Playboy, 1976.

Eisenhower, Dwight D. *At Ease: Stories I Tell My Friends*. Garden City, New York: Doubleday, 1967.

Sills, Beverly, and Larry Linderman. *Beverly: An Autobiography*. New York: Bantam, 1987.

Hatch, Alden. *A Man Named John: The Life of Pope John XXIII*. New York: Hawthorne, 1963.

Zimmer, Norma. *Norma*. Wheaton, Illinois: Tyndale, 1976.

Sharansky, Natan. *Fear No Evil*. Translated by Stefani Hoffman. New York: Random House, 1988.

Donovan, Roberta. Letter to author, 20 October 1988.

Petrakis, Harry Mark. *Reflections: A Writer's Life/A Writer's Work*. Chicago: Lake View, 1983.

Walesa, Lech. *A Way of Hope: An Autobiography*. New York: Henry Holt, 1987.

Linkletter, Art, with Dean Jennings. *Confessions of a Happy Man*. New York: Bernard Geis Associates, 1960.

Grizzard, Lewis, Jr. *My Daddy Was a Pistol and I'm a Son of a Gun*. New York: Villard Books, 1986.

Buechner, Frederick. *This Sacred Journey*. San Francisco: Harper and Row, 1982.

Koons, Carolyn. *Beyond Betrayal*. San Francisco: Harper and Row, 1986.

Hansel, Tim. *You Gotta Keep Dancin'*. Chicago: David C. Cook, 1985.

Worship in Song: A Hymnal. Kansas City, Missouri: Lillenas Publishing House, 1972.

Geffin, Roger. *The Handbook of Public Prayer.* New York: Macmillan, 1963.

Schuller, Robert H. *Prayers for Power-Filled Living.* New York: Hawthorne, 1976.

Chapter 2

Petrakis, Harry Mark. *Reflections: A Writer's Life/A Writer's Work.* Chicago: Lake View, 1983.

Falwell, Jerry. *Strength for the Journey.* New York: Simon and Schuster, 1987.

Grizzard, Lewis, Jr. *My Daddy Was a Pistol and I'm a Son of a Gun.* New York: Villard Books, 1986.

Wilkins, Roger. *A Man's Life: An Autobiography.* New York: Simon and Schuster, 1982.

Graziano, Rocky. *Somebody up There Likes Me—The Story of My Life So Far.* New York: Simon and Schuster, 1955.

Caro, Robert A. *The Years of Lyndon Johnson: The Path to Power.* New York: Knopf, 1982.

Sharansky, Natan. *Fear No Evil.* Translated by Stefani Hoffman. New York: Random House, 1988.

Worship in Song: A Hymnal. Kansas City, Missouri: Lillenas Publishing House, 1972.

Chapter 3

Peale, Norman Vincent. *The Healing of Sorrow.* Pawling, New York: Inspiration Book Service, 1966.

Manning, Doug. *Don't Take My Grief Away: What to Do When You Lose a Loved One.* San Francisco: Harper and Row, 1984.

Harbaugh, William Henry. *Power and Responsibility: The Life and Times of Theodore Roosevelt.* New York: Farrar, Straus and Cudahy, 1961.

Carter, Violet Bonham. *Winston Churchill: An Intimate Portrait.* New York: Harcourt, Brace and World, 1965.

Benson, Robert, ed. *See You at the House: The Stories Bob Benson Used To Tell.* Nashville: Generoux, 1986.

Manning, Doug. *Don't Take My Grief Away: What to Do When You Lose a Loved One.* San Francisco: Harper and Row, 1984.

Worship in Song: A Hymnal. Kansas City, Missouri: Lillenas Publishing House, 1972.

Barrows, Cliff, ed., *Crusader Hymns and Hymn Stories.* Special Crusade Edition. Chicago: Hope, 1967.

Book of Common Prayer and Administration of the Sacraments and Other Rites and Ceremonies of the Church. New York: Seabury Press, 1979.

Barclay, William. *Prayers for Help and Healing.* New York: Harper and Row, 1968.

Bush, George. "Saturday Journal." *The New Haven Register,* 17 June 1972, 16.

ten Boom, Corrie. *A Prisoner and Yet.* Harrisonburg, Virginia: Christian Light, 1964.

Sills, Beverly, and Larry Linderman. *Beverly. An Autobiography.* New York: Bantam, 1987.

Dobson, James, Jr. "Tribute to My Father." *Herald of Holiness,* 15 June 1978, 20–21.

Gordon, Mary. "Getting Here from There." in *Spiritual Quests,* edited by William Zinsser. Boston: Houghton Mifflin, 1988.

White, William Allen. *The Autobiography of William Allen White.* New York: Macmillan, 1946.

Meir, Golda. *A Land of Our Own: An Oral Autobiography.* Edited by Marie Syrkin. New York: Putnam, 1973.

Iacocca, Lee, with William Novak. *Iacocca: An Autobiography.* New York: Bantam, 1984.

Hilton, Stanley G. *Bob Dole: American Political Phoenix.* New York: Contemporary, 1988.

Hammer, Armand, with Neil Lyman. *Hammer.* New York: Putnam, 1987.

"Carl Lewis' Father. "*Jet,* 25 May 1987, 50.

Manning, Doug. *Don't Take My Grief Away: What to Do When You Lose a Loved One.* San Francisco: Harper and Row, 1984.

Benson, Robert, ed. *See You at the House: The Stories Bob Benson Used To Tell.* Nashville: Generoux, 1986.

Wallis, Charles L., ed. *The Funeral Encyclopedia: A Source Book.* New York: Harper and Brothers, 1953.

Castle, Tony, ed. *The New Book of Christian Prayers.* New York: Cross-roads, 1986.

Geffin, Roger. *The Handbook of Public Prayer.* New York: Macmillan, 1963.

Bibliography

Bradley, David. "Bringing Down the Fire." In *Spiritual Quests,* edited by William Zinsser. Boston: Houghton Mifflin, 1988.

Bush, George. Letter to author, 31 October 1988.

Bush, George, with Victor Gold. *Looking Forward.* New York: Doubleday, 1987.

Coffin, William Sloan. "Death: More Friend Than Foe." *The Christian Ministry,* 16 May 1985, 5.

Forbes, Malcolm. *They Went That-a-Way.* New York: Simon and Schuster, 1988.

Ford, Leighton. *Sandy: A Heart for God.* Downers Grove, Illinois: InterVarsity, 1985.

Graham, Otis L., Jr., and Meghan Robinson Wander, eds. *Franklin D. Roosevelt: His Life and Times, An Encyclopedic View.* Boston: G. K. Hall, 1985.

Grollman, Earl A. *Talking about Death: A Dialogue between Parent and Child.* Boston: Beacon, 1976.

Kreeft, Peter. *Making Sense Out of Suffering.* Ann Arbor, Michigan: 1986.

_____. *A Turn of the Clock: A Book of Modern Proverbs.* San Francisco: Ignatius, 1987.

Ladra, Michael. "Help from Heaven for the Dying." *Christian Reader,* 5 May 1988, 53–55.

[Moody, Dwight L.] "The Founding of Moody Institute." *Moody Monthly,* February 1985, 32.

Moore, Kenny. "Man, Not Superman." *Sports Illustrated,* 10 October 1988, 50–55.

"More on Carl Lewis." *Jet,* 1 June 1987, 50.

Peale, Norman. Letter to author, 29 November 1988.

"The Quiet People of Christmas." *Guideposts,* December 1985, 16–17.

Smith, Harold Ivan. "A Tribute to Dad." *Herald of Holiness,* 15 June 1981, 5–6.

Quotation Resources

Church, F. Forrester. *Father and Son: A Personal Biography.* New York: Morrow, 1988.

Edwards, Tryon. *The New Dictionary of Thoughts: A Cyclopedia of Quotations* Rev. ed. edited by Ralph Emerson Browns. New York: Standard, 1966.

Goudge, Elizabeth. *A Book of Comfort.* New York: Coward-McCann, 1964.

Kushner, Harold. *When All You've Ever Wanted Isn't Enough.* New York: Summit, 1986.

Roberts, Kate Louise, ed. *Hoyt's New Cyclopedia of Practical Quotations.* New York: Funk and Wagnalls, 1927.

Prayer Resources

Baird, William R., Sr., and John E. Baird. *Funeral Meditations.* Nashville: Abingdon, 1966.

Barclay, William. *Prayers for Help and Healing.* New York: Harper and Row, 1968.

Book of Common Prayer and Administration of the Sacraments and Other Rites and Ceremonies of the Church. New York: Seabury Press, 1979.

Castle, Tony, ed. *The New Book of Christian Prayers.* New York: Crossroads, 1986.

Fosdick, Harry Emerson. *A Book of Public Prayers.* New York: Harper and Brothers, 1959.

Geffin, Roger. *The Handbook of Public Prayer.* New York: Macmillan, 1963.

Lerach, William H., ed. *The Improved Funeral Manual.* New York: Revell, 1942.

Miller, Samuel H. *Prayers for Daily Use.* New York: Harper and Brothers, 1957.

Powell, Paul. *Gospel from the Graveside.* Self-published, 1981.

Prayers for All Occasions. Grand Rapids, Michigan: Baker, 1960.

Schuller, Robert H. *Prayers for Power-Filled Living.* New York: Hawthorne, 1976.

Wallis, Charles L., ed. *The Funeral Encyclopedia: A Source Book.* New York: Harper and Brothers, 1953.

Worship in Song: A Hymnal. Kansas City, Missouri: Lillenas Publishing House, 1972.

For information on the ministry of
Harold Ivan Smith please contact:
Harold Ivan Smith
P.O. Box 24688
Kansas City, MO 64131